Royal Exchange Theatre & HighTide Festival Theatre
present

SO HERE WE ARE

BY LUKE NORRIS

So Here We Are premiered at the 2015 HighTide Festival,
Aldeburgh, on 10 September 2015

The production transferred to the Royal Exchange Theatre,
Manchester, on 24 September 2015

SO HERE WE ARE

BY LUKE NORRIS

KIRSTY	Jade Anouka
FRANKIE	Daniel Kendrick
PIDGE	Sam Melvin
DAN	Ciarán Owens
SMUDGE	Dorian Jerome Simpson
PUGH	Mark Weinman

DIRECTOR	Steven Atkinson
DESIGNER	Lily Arnold
LIGHTING	Katharine Williams
COMPOSER AND SOUND	Isobel Waller-Bridge
MOVEMENT DIRECTOR	Tom Jackson Greaves
CASTING DIRECTOR	Jerry Knight-Smith CDG
ASSISTANT DIRECTOR	Piers Black-Hawkins
STAGE MANAGER	Harriet Stewart
DEPUTY STAGE MANAGER	Philip Hussey

THE COMPANY

JADE ANOUKA (Kirsty) is making her Royal Exchange Theatre debut. Other theatre includes: *Chef* (Soho/Edinburgh Festival); *The Vote, Henry IV* (Donmar Warehouse); *Omeros* (Sam Wanamaker); *Julius Caesar* (Donmar/St Ann's Warehouse, New York); *Clean* (Traverse/59E59, New York); *Romeo and Juliet* (Shakespeare's Globe/UAE tour); *Moon on a Rainbow Shawl* (National Theatre); *Hamlet* (Shakespeare's Globe/European tour); *Romeo and Juliet* (Bolton Octagon); *Wild Horses* (Theatre503); *Love's Labour's Lost* (Shakespeare's Globe/US tour); *Blood Wedding* (Southwark Playhouse); *Twelfth Night* (York Theatre Royal); *The Merchant of Venice, The Taming of the Shrew, The Penelopiad* (RSC); *Dick Whittington, Golden Boy* (Greenwich); *Handa's Surprise* (Little Angel); *Unstoned, Outright Terror Bold & Brilliant* (Soho). Film credits include: *A Running Jump; A Summer Hamlet, The Dark Channel*. Television credits include: *Lucky Man; Doctor Who; Shakespeare Uncovered; Secrets and Words; Law & Order UK, USS Constellation*.

DANIEL KENDRICK (Frankie) is making his first appearance for the Royal Exchange Theatre. Other theatre credits include: *Our Town* (Almeida); *Ding Dong the Wicked, Vera Vera Vera, If You Don't Let Us Dream, We Won't Let You Sleep* (Royal Court); *Rosie & Jim* (Mobculture); *Chapel Street* (Old Red Lion/Liverpool Playhouse) and *Coalition* (Theatre503). Television credits include: *Black Mirror; Ripper Street; Our World War; Mr Selfridge 2; Run* and *EastEnders*. Film credits include: *Us and Them; Offender* and *Love Bite*.

SAM MELVIN (Pidge) is making his first appearance for the Royal Exchange Theatre and his stage debut. Sam trained at the Oxford School of Drama. Training credits include: *Anna Karenina* (Royal Court); *Black Sheep* (Soho). Television credits include: *From the Cradle to the Grave; EastEnders; Casualty* and *MI High*.

CIARÁN OWENS (Dan) is making his first appearance for the Royal Exchange Theatre. Theatre credits include: *The Crocodile* (Manchester International Festival); *King John* (Shakespeare's Globe); *A Handful of Stars* (Trafalgar Studios/Theatre503); *Oh! What A Lovely War* (Theatre Royal, Stratford East); *Candide, Titus Andronicus, A Mad World My Masters* (RSC); *Our Country's Good* (Out of John), *Mercury Fur* (Trafalgar Studios); *A Butcher of Distinction* (The King's Head); *Eye/Balls, Eating Ice Cream on Gaza Beach, White Boy, Victory Street, Still Killing Time* (Soho). Television credits include: *Arthur and George; Spotless; Wallander* and *The Inbetweeners*.

DORIAN JEROME SIMPSON (Smudge) is making his first appearance for the Royal Exchange Theatre. Dorian trained at Royal Welsh College of Music and Drama. Training credits include: *The Lower Depths, Anne Boleyn, Incomplete and Random Acts of Kindness, Pericles, A Month in the Country, Beasts and the Beauties, Earthquakes in London* and *King Lear*. Theatre credits include: *Sherman Swingers* (Sherman Cymru); *A Good Clean Heart* (Other Room Theatre). Film credits include: *The Guvnors; Turnout; Abusing Protocol, Shitkicker*. Television credits include: *Stella*.

MARK WEINMAN (Pugh) is making his first appearance for the Royal Exchange Theatre. Other theatre credits include: *Captain Amazing, Eating Ice Cream on Gaza Beach* (Soho); *Prime Time, Serjeant Musgrave's Dance* (Royal Court); *Herons* (Stephen Joseph/Manchester Library Theatre); *Fastburn* (KneeHigh); *The Hairy Ape* (Southwark Playhouse); *Nettles* (Contact Theatre);

Selling Clive (Lost Theatre); *Step 9 (of 12)* (New Britannia Theatre); *Barrow Hill* (Finborough); *The Emperor Jones* (National Theatre); *Captain Amazing* (Live Theatre); *Edmond* (Theatre Royal Haymarket/Masterclass); *Prophecy* (Baz Theatre); *Sandy 123* (The Roundhouse); *Amphibians* (Offstage Theatre) and *Sherlock Holmes* (Italian tour). Television credits include: *Game Changer, Humans, Episodes*. Film credits include: *Burning, Waves*.

LUKE NORRIS (Writer) is a writer and actor. Luke has acted at the Royal Exchange Theatre in *Orpheus Descending*. His writing credits include: *Growth* (Gate Theatre); *Hearts* (National Theatre Connections); *A Puzzle* (Site Specific piece for the Royal Court); *Goodbye To All That* (Jerwood Theatre Upstairs) and *Borough Market* (Edinburgh Fringe).

STEVEN ATKINSON (Director) is the co-founder and Artistic Director of HighTide Festival Theatre and is directing at the Royal Exchange for the first time. Steven's theatre credits for HighTide include: *Lampedusa* (Soho/HighTide Festival); *peddling* (Arcola/Off-Broadway/HighTide Festival); *Pussy Riot: Hunger Strike* (Bush/Southbank Centre); *Neighbors* (Nuffield/HighTide Festival); *Bottleneck* (Soho/HighTide Festival/UK tour); *Clockwork* (HighTide Festival); *Bethany* (HighTide Festival/Public Theater, New York); *Incoming* (Latitude Festival/HighTide Festival); *Dusk Rings A Bell* (Watford Palace Theatre/HighTide Festival); *Lidless* (Trafalgar Studios/HighTide Festival); *Muhmah* (HighTide Festival); *The Pitch* (Latitude Festival). Other directing credits include: *Chicken* (Eastern Angles/Paines Plough Roundabout); *Three Card Trick* (Liverpool Everyman & Playhouse); *The Afghan and the Penguin* (BBC Radio 4); *Freedom Trilogy* (Hull Truck Theatre); *Sexual Perversity in Chicago* (Edinburgh Festival).

LILY ARNOLD (Designer) trained at Wimbledon College of Arts. Theatre and opera credits include: *Things Will Never Be the Same Again* (Tricycle); *The Solid Life of Sugar Water* (Graeae); *The Jew of Malta, King Lear, The Taming of the Shrew, The Rape of Lucrece* (RSC); *Beached* (Marlow Studios/Soho); *The Edge of Our Bodies, Gruesome Playground Injuries* (Gate); *peddling* (HighTide); *Minotaur* (Polka); *World Enough and Time* (Park); *The Boss of it All* (Assembly Roxy/Soho); *A Season in Congo, The Scottboro Boys* (Young Vic); *Happy New* (Trafalgar Studios); *Ahasverus* (Hampstead Downstairs); *A Midsummer Night's Dream* (Cambridge Arts Theatre); *Opera Scenes* (National Opera Studio); *Red Handed* (The Place, London).

KATHARINE WILLIAMS (Lighting Designer) Theatre credits include: *Care* (Tangled Feet); *Adriano in Siria* (Classical Opera); *You Have Been Upgraded* (Science Museum); *Get Santa!* (Northern Stage); *Am I Dead Yet?, The Noise* (Unlimited Theatre); *Bluebeard's Castle* (Opera Oviedo); *Stowaway* (Analogue Productions); *Men in the Cities* (Chris Goode & Company); *Dealer's Choice* (Royal & Derngate); *Mad Man* (Plymouth Theatre Royal); *Billy the Girl* (Clean Break); *Moominland Winter* (Theatre Royal Bath); *Medea* (Actors of Dionysus); *The Ruling Class* (English Theatre Frankfurt); *A Midsummer Night's Dream, Cyrano De Bergerac, Othello* (Grosvenor Park Open Air Theatre); *Address Unknown* (Soho); *Not I* (Royal Court); *Say It With Flowers* (Sherman Cymru); *Resonance at the Still Point of Change* (Southbank Centre); *Heidi – A Goat's Tail* (Theatre Royal Bath); *Ballroom of Joy and Sorrows* (Watford Palace Theatre); *Krapp's Last Tape/ Spoonface Steinberg* (Hull Truck); *Anne and Zef* (Company of Angels); *God/Head* (Chris Goode & Company); *The French Detective and the Blue Dog* (Bath Theatre Royal); *The Westbridge* (Royal Court); *Invisible* (Transport); *The Pajama Men* (Assembly Theatre); *Closer* (Théâtre des Capucins); *Faeries* (Royal Opera House); *Landscape & Monologue* (Theatre Royal Bath); *Ivan and the Dogs*

(ATC/Soho); *The Goat, Or Who is Sylvia?* (Traverse); *Reykjavic* (Shams); *Nocturnal* (The Gate); *Amgen:Broken* (Sherman Cymru/Theatr Clywd); *Dolls* (National Theatre of Scotland); *I Am Falling* (Gate/Sadler's Wells); *Touched for the Very First Time* (Trafalgar Studios).

ISOBEL WALLER-BRIDGE (Composer and Sound Designer) Music for theatre includes, as Composer and Sound Designer: *Incognito* (HighTide/ Bush); *Not the Worst Place* (Sherman Cymru); *Yellow Face* (The Shed at the National Theatre); *Fleabag* (Soho); *Orlando, Billy Liar* (Royal Exchange Theatre); *The Ideal World season* (Watford Palace Theatre); *Forever House* (Theatre Royal Plymouth); *Sleuth* (Watermill); *Mydidae* (Soho); *Gruesome Playground Injuries* (Gate); *The Girl With the Iron Claws* (Soho); *Head/Heart* (Bristol Tobacco Factory); *Blink* (Traverse/Soho); *By the Bog of Cats* (Abbey); *Lampedusa* (HighTide/Soho); *Posh* (Nottingham Playhouse/Salisbury Arts Theatre); *Exit the King* (Bath Theatre Royal); *Uncle Vanya* (St James/Jagged Fence). As Composer: *Hope Place* (Liverpool Everyman); *King Lear, Neville's Island* (Chichester Festival Theatre); *If Only* (Minerva); *The Hook* (Royal & Derngate). Music for film, TV & radio includes, as Composer: *James* (Wellcome Trust); *Tracks* (Rankin/ Collabor8te); *The Frozen Planet: Freeze Frames* (BBC); *Secret Symphony* (Samsung/ The Times; *Gilead* (Radio 3); *Tracks* (short); *Physics* (winner of LFC Best of Boroughs 2012 @ BFI) (short); *Ellie* (short); *Disaffected* (short); *Beautiful Enough* (short); *Hometown* (short); *Meeting Mr Tiller* (short). As Orchestrator/ Arranger: *The Whale* (BBC/Discovery); *The Imposter* (Film 4); *Life* (BBC); *Planet Earth Live!* (BBC); *The Bounty Hunter* (Columbia Pictures); *The Day of the Flowers* (dir. John Roberts); *Route Irish* (Sixteen Films); *Concert for Care 2013* (Royal Albert Hall); *Masters of Film Music* (Dallas Symphony Orchestra). As Musical Director: *The Boy I Love* (V&A); *A Woman Killed With Kindness* (National Theatre); *A Christmas Carol* (Lowry Theatre). Other projects include an opera based on Angela Carter's short stories, *The Bloody Chamber*.

TOM JACKSON GREAVES (Movement Director) is a choreographer and movement director. Previous choreographic work includes: *The Glass Menagerie* (Headlong Theatre UK tour); *Juicy and Delicious* (Nuffield Theatre Southampton); *When We Were Women* (The Orange Tree); *The Crocodile* (Manchester International Festival); *Teddy* (Southwark Playhouse); *Defect The Musical* (Arts Ed); *Shadowthief* (Barnsley Civic); *Kerry Ellis at The Palladium* (London Palladium), *Lift The Musical* (Soho); *Harvest Fire* (YMT The Lemon Tree Aberdeen); *The Seventh Muse* (YMT Barbican Plymouth) and music videos for Boy George and Clare Maguire. Tom also creates his own dance-theatre work including: *Seven Deadly Sins* (UK tour) and *Vanity Fowl* (Sadler's Wells). Tom was a winner of the New Adventures Choreographer Award in 2012. Tom has also worked extensively as a performer touring regularly with 'Matthew Bourne's New Adventures'. Other highlights include: *Tristan And Yseult* (Kneehigh Theatre) and *Kes* (Sheffield Crucible).

PIERS BLACK-HAWKINS (Assistant Director) is a director, writer and co-founder of Ransack Theatre. Previous directing credits include: *Come Closer* (Royal Exchange); *The Dumb Waiter* (re:play at HOME, NSDF and Lucy Davis Vaults) and *Solve* (Edinburgh Festival). Previous assistant directing credits include *Yen* (Royal Exchange Theatre). Piers has also worked with the Soho Theatre, Tricycle Theatre, HighTide and Bolton Octagon alongside further work with the Royal Exchange, HOME and Ransack.

Situated in the heart of Manchester, the Royal Exchange Theatre is one of the UK's leading producing theatres. We showcase an ambitious programme inspired by the world's greatest stories: stories that have the power to change the way we see the world. To us, that means taking artistic risks, working as part of exciting partnerships, championing new talent and seeking out bold collaborations. A record number of people have experienced our work in the last year, and we're continuing to broaden our output on and off our stages to speak to the most diverse audiences in Manchester and beyond.

We're committed to supporting and developing new writing. The Bruntwood Prize for Playwriting is the UK's biggest playwriting competition and celebrates its 10th anniversary this year. *So Here We Are* was winner of the 2013 Judges Award, and this season also saw successful productions of 2013 Bruntwood Prize Winners *Yen* by Anna Jordan, and *The Rolling Stone* by Chris Urch.

Forthcoming productions include a co-production of the Orange Tree Theatre's *Pomona* with the National Theatre, written by Alistair McDowall (author of the Bruntwood Prize winning *Brilliant Adventures*). Our association with the National Theatre continues with *Husbands And Sons*, directed by Marianne Elliott which will transfer from the National at the opening of our Spring Summer 2016 Season.

The Great Hall of the Royal Exchange

To find out more please visit www.royalexchange.co.uk, or follow us twitter.com/rxtheatre
Box Office 0161 833 9833

Registered Charity Number 255424

ROYAL EXCHANGE THEATRE STAFF

ROYAL EXCHANGE THEATRE STAFF

Box Office
Box Office Manager
Sue Partington
Deputy Box Office Manager Wendy Miller
Box Office Assistants
William Barnett,
Jon Brennan, Lindsay Burke,
Dan Glynn, Zoe Nicholas,
Christine Simpson,
Eleanor Walk

Casting
Casting Director & Associate Director
Jerry Knight-Smith CDG

Catering
Bar Manager Chris Wilson
Café Manager
Kieron Carney
Restaurant Manager
Emma Gold
General Manager
Leigh Edmondson
Events & Hospitality Manager Jake Tysome
Head Chef
Chris Watson-Gunby
Bar & Catering Staff
Mohammed Ahmed,
Jill Angel, Chloe Baulcombe,
Mark Beattie, Cat Belcher,
Hannah Blakely, Mazz Brown,
Paul Callaghan, Leah Curran,
Scott Foulds, Jake Gamble,
Chris Gray, Abigail Henshaw,
Amy Lawrence, Simon Mayne,
Rafal Michnikowski, Chloe
Nugent, Jenny Nuttall,
Matt Nutter, Tom Redshaw,
Paul Roberts, Mark Smith,
Camille Smithwick

Company
Company Manager
Lee Drinkwater

Costume Hire
Costume Hire Manager
Ludmila Krzak
Acting Craft Shop Manager Gail Myerscough
Acting Assistant Manager
Clare Sidebotham
Assistants Sarah Malone,
Elisa Robertson, Amber
Samuels, Emily Tilzey, Frankii
Tonge

Development
Development Director
Val Young
Senior Development Manager Gina Fletcher
Development Managers
Becky Rosenthal,
Gemma Snow
Development Executive
Holli Leah
Friends Organiser
Kate Hollier

Directorate
Artistic Director
Sarah Frankcom
Associate Artistic Director Matthew Xia
Associate Artists
Maxine Peake, Benji Reid,
Chris Thorpe

Birkbeck Associate
Kate Colgrave-Pope
Executive Director
Fiona Gasper
Director of Engagement
Amanda Dalton
Senior Producer
Richard Morgan
Producer Amy Clewes
Assistant to the Artistic Directors & Senior Producer Michelle Hickman
Assistant to the Executive Director & Director of Finance & Admin
Jan-Louise Blyth

Finance & Administration
Director of Finance & Administration Barry James
HR Manager Yvonne Cox
Accounts Manager
Lesley Farthing
Orders & Purchase Ledger Clerk Jennifer Ellis
Payroll Clerk Carl Robson

Green Room
Supervisor Yvonne Stott
Assistant Anne Dardis

Information Technology
IT Manager Ean Burgon
IT Apprentice Zak Clifford

Literary & Talent Development
New Writing Associate
Suzanne Bell
Bruntwood Hub Associate Playwright Bryony Lavery
Hub Salon Playwrights
Katie Douglas, Aisha Khan,
Lee Mattinson, Alistair
McDowell, Lizzie Nunnery,
Ben Tagoe, Tom Wells
Writer on Attachment
David Judge (Talawa Writers
Programme funded by Paul
Hamlyn Foundation)
Literary & Talent Development Assistant
Davinia Jokhi

Lighting
Acting Head of Lighting
Mark Distin
Senior Technicians Alex
Dixon, Matt Lever
Technician Alex Pullen

Marketing
Acting Director of Marketing & Communications
Vanessa Walters
Design & Print Manager
Maxine Laing
Communications Manager Paula Rabbitt
Marketing Officer – Digital & Systems
Vicky Bloor
Marketing Officer – Groups Eleanor Higgins
Marketing Officer
Anneka Morley
Marketing Assistant
Ashley McKay
Archivist (Volunteer)
Stella Lowe

Participation & Learning
Head of Participation & Learning Sarah Lovell
Producer – Creative Industry Experience
Chris Wright
Producer – Special Projects Kate Reynolds
Adults Programme Leader Andy Barry
Community Programme Leader Tracie Daly
Schools' Programme Leader Natalie Diddams
Young People's Programme Leader
Matt Hassall
Truth About Youth Associate Alex Summers
Administrator
Emma Wallace
Participation & Learning Administration Assistant
Katherine de Val

Production
Head of Production
Simon Curtis
Production Co-ordinator
Greg Skipworth
Props Buyer Kim Ford
Driver John Fisher
Props & Settings
Head of Props & Settings
Neil Gidley
Deputy Heads of Props & Settings Andrew Bubble,
Senior Scenic Artist
Philip Costello
Prop Makers Carl Heston,
Stephen Lafferty, Stuart
Mitchell, Meriel Pym, Sarah
Worrall
Props & Settings Intern
Jo Myers

Sound
Acting Head of Sound
Sorcha Williams
Senior Technician
David Norton, Ben Almond
Stage Technicians
Technical Stage Manager
Andy Roberts
Technicians Luke Murray,
Simon Wild

Visitor Experience & Operations
Operations Director
Jo Topping
Visitor Experience Manager Lynne Yates
Deputy Visitor Experience Manager Stuart Galligan
Facilities Manager
David Mitchell
Maintenance Technician
Rodney Bostock
Hire & Events Assistant
Jenny Graham
Relief FOH Managers
Jill Bridgman, Rachel Davies,
Julian Kelly, Stuart Shaw
Relief Deputy Managers
Helen Coyne, Chris Dance,
Dan Glynn
Security Liam Carty, David
Hughes, Mike Seal

Stage Door Thomas Flaherty,
Peter Mainka, Laurence
McBride
Head Cleaner
Lillian Williams
Cleaners Gillian Bradshaw,
Susan Burrough, Elaine
Connolly, Valarie Daffern,
Jacqueline Donohue,
Elizabeth Farrell, Ahab
Mohamed, Lillian Williams
Ushers Liam Ainsworth, Tom
Banks, Jill Bridgman, Georgie
Brown, Sarah Button, Natasha
Bybik, Elizabeth Callan, Liam
Carty, Richard Challinore, Liz
Coupe, Helen Coyne, Chris
Dance, Anna Davenport,
Rachel Davies, Harriet Eakin,
Luther Edmead, Paul Evans,
Neil Fenton, Beth Galligan,
Dan Glynn, Lucy Hayes, Sarah
Hill, Jen Hulman, Julian Kelly,
Dan Lizar, Heather Madden,
Tony O'Driscoll, Annie
Roberts, Mike Seal, Stuart
Shaw, Eleanor Theodorou,
Vincent Tuohy, Ted Walker,
Judith Wood, Mahdi Zadeh

Wardrobe
Head of Wardrobe
Nicola Meredith
Deputy Head of Wardrobe Tracey Dunk
Studio Wardrobe Supervisor Felicia Jagne
Cutters Rachel Bailey,
Jennifer Adgey
Tailor & Gents Cutter
Rose Calderbank
Wardrobe Maintenance Mistress Kate Elphick
Maintenance Wardrobe Assistant Michael Grant
Wigs, Hair & Make-up Supervisor Jo Shepstone
Wigs & Make-up Intern
Hira Qudoos

ROYAL EXCHANGE THEATRE

Patron HRH the Earl of Wessex CVO

THE BRUNTWOOD PRIZE FOR PLAYWRITING 2015

On 17 November the 2015 Bruntwood Prize for Playwriting will be awarded in a prizegiving ceremony taking place at the Royal Exchange Theatre.

This year's competition had a massive 1,938 entries, the second highest ever, with over 67% of entries from writers submitting for the very first time. A team of over 40 readers are currently reading each individual entry to create a long list of potential winners. In November a shortlist will be handed to this year's panel of judges chaired by **Sir Nicholas Hytner** and including journalist **Miranda Sawyer**, actor **Meera Syal**, and former Bruntwood Prize winner **Vivienne Franzmann**.

2015 is the 10th anniversary year of the Prize. Its incredible legacy has a truly global reach, and has kick-started the careers of some of the most significant writers working in British Theatre today – Duncan Macmillan, Vivienne Franzmann and Alistair McDowall. This year both *Yen* by Anna Jordan, the 2013 winner, and *The Rolling Stone* by Chris Urch, also a prize winner, played to amazing reviews and critical acclaim at the Royal Exchange Theatre and beyond.

'The Bruntwood Prize creates a pathway for anyone, regardless of whether they are already connected to theatre or not, to conceive and realise a play – this has been the DNA of the Prize since it started. The Prize and its extraordinary legacy would not be possible without Bruntwood's continued vision, which has facilitated its growth and has been tremendously supportive throughout its development. This year, the message was to 'Create Your Own Stage' – to be bold, to be brave, to think big – to give us something that we have never seen before, to respond to our times and to change the landscape of theatre as we know it. We can't wait to see how this year's entrants have responded' **Sarah Frankcom, Artistic Director**

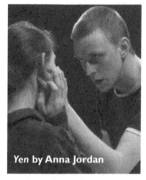

Yen by Anna Jordan

★★★★★ **Brutal and tender... Jordan's writing is extraordinary'** *Guardian*

The Rolling Stone by Chris Urch

★★★★★ **'This is a sublime play, a superb production... It demands to be seen'** **WhatsOnStage**

bruntwood ●

Royal Exchange Theatre

Autumn/Winter 2015/16 season at the Royal Exchange Theatre

THE CRUCIBLE
The Theatre Friday 18 September – Saturday 24 October
By Arthur Miller
Directed by Caroline Steinbeis

Orange Tree Theatre presents (in association with the National Theatre and the Royal Exchange Theatre)
POMONA
The Theatre Thursday 29 October – Saturday 21 November
By Alistair McDowall
Directed by Ned Bennett

INTO THE WOODS
The Theatre Friday 4 December – Saturday 16 January
Music and lyrics by Stephen Sondheim
Book by James Lapine
Directed by Matthew Xia

WIT
The Theatre Thursday 21 January – Saturday 13 February
By Margaret Edson
Directed by Raz Shaw
With Julie Hesmondhalgh

For more information or to book your tickets, call the Box Office on
0161 833 9833 or visit **royalexchange.co.uk**

Why not save 20% by purchasing a season ticket?!
Full details at **royalexchange.co.uk/seasontickets**

HighTide Festival Theatre

"HighTide has a deserved reputation as an exciting home for new playwriting." Sunday Times

HighTide Festival Theatre, one of the UK's leading theatre companies, is focused on the production of new plays and developing emerging playwrights. Our core work is producing an annual festival in Suffolk of world and UK première productions. We have a national and international profile by touring new productions to some of the world's leading theatres.

Led since 2007 by co-founding Artistic Director Steven Atkinson, we have premièred over fifty major productions by playwrights including Adam Brace, Luke Barnes, Elinor Cook, E V Crowe, Ella Hickson, Sam Holcroft, Joel Horwood, Anders Lustgarten, Vinay Patel, Nick Payne, Jack Thorne and Frances Ya-Chu Cowhig.

Every script that we receive from around the world is read by our Artistic Director and Associates. The most promising of these playwrights occupy HighTide's year-round artistic development work, from workshops to full productions. Lansons host our administrative offices in-kind within their Clerkenwell offices in a multi-award winning partnership between a private business and an arts charity.

HighTide Festival Theatre is a National Portfolio Organisation of Arts Council England.

HT
2015

Our ninth Season commenced with the transfer of Vinay Patel's **True Brits** to London's VAULT Festival. Harry Melling's debut play **peddling** transferred to the Arcola Theatre following its run Off-Broadway and in HighTide Festival 2014.

Anders Lustgarten's **Lampedusa** premiered at Soho Theatre ahead of its transfer to HighTide Festival 2015 and Unity Theatre, Liverpool.

HighTide Festival 2015 will premiere new productions by E V Crowe, Anders Lustgarten, Luke Norris and Al Smith, and Artist Talks with Christopher Eccleston,

Richard Eyre, Meera Syal and Vanessa Redgrave.

Luke Norris's Bruntwood Prize-winning play **So Here We Are** will premiere at HighTide Festival 2015 ahead of transferring to the Royal Exchange Theatre, Manchester.

E V Crowe's **BRENDA** will premiere at HighTide Festival 2015 ahead of transferring to The Yard Theatre, London.

Tom Holloway's **Forget Me Not** will receive its European Premiere at the Bush Theatre in December 2015.

For full details please visit www.hightide.org.uk

Image: *Incognito* by Nick Payne (HighTide 2014)
Photographer: Bill Knight

HighTide Festival Theatre

24a St John Street, London, EC1M 4AY
0207 566 9765 : hello@hightide.org.uk : www.hightide.org.uk

HighTide Company

Artistic Director – Steven Atkinson
Executive Director – Holly Kendrick
Producer – Francesca Clark
Marketing and Development Officer – Freddie Porter
Festival General Manager – Joshua McTaggart
Literary Associate – Stephanie Street
Resident Writer – Melanie Spencer

Marketing and Press

Marketing Consultant – JHI – 020 7420 7730
Marketing Design – Chris Perkin
Press – Dee McCourt and Giles Cooper for Borkowski Arts & Ents 020 3176 2700

Artistic Associates

Nadia Albina, Tom Attenborough, Justin Audibert, Richard Beecham, George Chilcott, Ella
Hickson, Paul Jellis, Zoe Lewis, Emily Lim, Caitlin McLeod, Prasanna Puwanarajah, Chris Thorpe,
Will Wrightson

Playwrights-on-Attachment

Georgia Christou, Vickie Donoghue, Marcelo Dos Santos, Louise Gooding, Daniel Kanaber,
Nessah Muthy, Vinay Patel, Sophie Stanton

In 2014-15 HighTide has collaborated with:

Southbank Centre; Soho Theatre; Theatre Royal Bath; nabakov; Live Theatre, Newcastle; North
Wall, Oxford; 59E59, New York City; Ideas Tap; Bush Theatre; Nuffield, Southampton; Royal &
Derngate, Northampton; Underbelly, Edinburgh; Pleasance, Edinburgh; The Garage, Norwich;
VAULT Festival; Arcola Theatre; Chichester Festival Theatre; Unity Theatre; Royal Exchange
Theatre; The Yard Theatre

Board

Steven Atkinson, Amy Bird, Peter Clayton,
Sue Emmas, Nick Giles, Diana Hiddleston,
Mark Lacey, Criona Palmer, Clare Parsons,
Tali Pelman, Dallas Smith, Graham White,
Peter Wilson MBE (Chair)

Advisory Council

Jack Bradley, Robert Fox, Thelma Holt CBE,
Mel Kenyon, Tom Morris, Roger Wingate

Patrons

Sinead Cusack, Stephen Daldry CBE,
Sir Richard Eyre CBE, Sally Greene OBE,
Sir David Hare, Sir Nicholas Hytner, Sam
Mendes CBE, Juliet Stevenson CBE

Fidelio Charitable Trust, Martin Bowley Charitable Trust, Ronald Duncan Literary Foundation, Scarfe Charitable Trust

Support HighTide

HighTide Festival Theatre is a registered charity and every year the generosity of individuals, corporate sponsors, public funders, trusts and foundations enable us to create our award-winning artistic programme and grow our work for young people.

Donate to HighTide:

If you enjoy our work and would like to support us, then why not make a donation? Your support will help us to continue discovering, producing and championing the most promising emerging playwights.

To donate online please visit: www.hightide.org.uk/donate

Trusts and Foundations:

There are very talented young playwrights working in the UK, and if they are lucky they will find their way to the HighTide Festival Theatre season in Suffolk. I hope you will join me in supporting this remarkable and modest organisation. With your help HighTide can play an even more major role in promoting of new writing in the UK. (Lady Susie Sainsbury, Backstage Trust)

We have important partnerships with trusts, foundations and public funders who support our ambition and excellence, allowing us to deliver a wealth of opportunities for practitioners and participants alike. Working with our supporters we are committed to developing the next generation of artists and audiences.

We are supported by the following Trusts and Foundations

Lansons, Backstage Trust, Adnams Charity, Britten-Pears Foundation, Esmée Fairbairn Foundation, Fidelio Charitable Trust, Foyle Foundation, Garfield Weston Foundation, Harold Hyam Wingate Foundation, Mackintosh Foundation, Martin Bowley Charitable Trust, The Noël Coward Foundation, The Old Possum's Practical Trust, Parham Trust, The Richard Carne Trust, Ronald Duncan Literary Foundation, Scarfe Charitable Trust.

Business Sponsorship

We have worked with corporate partners: AEM International, Best of Suffolk, John Clayton & Bishops Printers, CMS Cameron McKenna, Lansons, JHI Marketing, Northern Trust, Suffolk Cottage Holidays. TA Hotel Collection, The Agency, United Agents.

Major Donors

Peter Fincham, Sam Fogg, Sir David Hare, Diana Hiddlestone, Clare Parsons and Tony Langham, Tony Mackintosh and Criona Palmer, Lady Susie Sainsbury, Albert and Marjorie Scardino, Rosemary Squire OBE.

Friends of HighTide

Alan Brodie, Sir David Green KCMG, Leah Scmidt.

To discuss supporting HighTide please contact Freddie Porter: **freddie@hightide.org.uk**

SO HERE WE ARE

Luke Norris

For the boys back home

Acknowledgements

Thanks to Leo Butler and all involved with the Royal Court 'Super-Group' 2012, where this play started its life.

Thanks to the myriad actors and directors who have read and noted it since then.

Thanks to all involved with the Bruntwood Prize and the Royal Exchange for bringing *So Here We Are* to light. Particular thanks go to Suz Bell for her continued interrogation of the text.

Thanks to Steven Atkinson and everyone at HighTide for committing to the production from first to last.

Thanks to Ciarán, Danny, Dorian, Jade, Mark and Sam for wanting to come along and tell the story with us.

Thanks to Jonathan Kinnersley for his unwavering faith and support.

And thanks, as ever, to my wife and (unpaid) dramaturg Jo, for everything.

L.N.

And the days are not full enough
And the nights are not full enough
And life slips by like a field mouse
Not shaking the grass.

Ezra Pound

Characters

PIDGE
SMUDGE
PUGH
DAN
KIRSTY
FRANKIE

This text went to press before the end of rehearsals and so may differ slightly from the play as performed.

A Note on the Punctuation

It's a bit of a mess.

Generally speaking, speeches should come quickly one after the next. To indicate and encourage this, a lot of speeches are written without full stops, whether the character has finished speaking or not.

Full stops, meanwhile, don't necessarily mean the end of a thought. Sometimes they do. But. Sometimes they just indicate a hiatus.

Forward slashes (/) within speeches indicate the point at which the next character starts speaking.

Brackets ( ) indicate *sotto voce*.

An ellipsis (…) in place of a speech indicates a pressure or an attempt to speak.

Beats are of varying length, relative to the pace of the scene. Long beats are longer. Obviously. Silences are longer still.

A question without a question mark indicates a flatness of tone.

I think that's it.

It's probably not.

PART ONE

Southend, Essex.

A milk-white day at the arse-end of summer.

SMUDGE *and* PUGH *sit high up on the crumbling, graffiti-daubed sea wall.* PIDGE *stands between them, wearing a surgical eyepatch.*

DAN *stands below on the sand/shingle, smoking a cigarette.*

All are mid-twenties and are dressed in variations of black suits with ties (except SMUDGE *who is in a short-sleeved shirt with no jacket). They each have a beer.*

A long silence – as long as we can get away with – as they look out at the water.

The occasional swig of beer.

Nothingness.

PIDGE *looks around at the other boys.*

One. Two. Three. And himself.

Beat.

PIDGE. Well he's fucked up the five-a-side, en e?

SMUDGE *and* PUGH *laugh/smile. To acknowledge the joke more than anything.* DAN *doesn't react.*

Silence again.

What time is it now?

No one responds.

Beat.

PIDGE *takes out his phone and checks the time, puts it away again.*

Beat.

She wants to hurry up, I need a shit

PUGH. Nice

SMUDGE. I could do with / a poo

PIDGE. I've already had two, it's that fuckin coffee

SMUDGE. I ain't bin all day

PUGH. What / coffee?

SMUDGE. I think it's the stress

PIDGE. I had a double expresso this mornin before I et anyfin.

PUGH. Espresso.

PIDGE. You what?

PUGH. Espresso. Not expresso

PIDGE. Yeah that's what I said, espresso.

PUGH. Alright

PIDGE. Na I did

PUGH. Alright

PIDGE. I fuckin did, Smudge didn't I say?

SMUDGE. I dint fink you drinked coffee?

PIDGE. Na well I don't do I cos it makes me shit.

PUGH. Makes you talk shit

SMUDGE. Then why'd you have one?

PIDGE. I dunno I thought it might gissa bit of summink, help us out or whatever like, I dunno

PUGH. You should've had your spinach.

PIDGE. My what?

PUGH. Your spinach.

PIDGE. What the fuck are you on about?

SMUDGE. Spinach

PUGH. Popeye

PIDGE. Popeye?

PUGH. Popeye, spinach

SMUDGE. Oh / yeah

PIDGE. Popeye yer fuckin – don't start all that again

PUGH. Aye aye

PIDGE. Oi I mean it I'm tryin to have a serious conversation here / yer cunt

PUGH. About how coffee makes you poo!

PIDGE. About how putting a mate in the ground takes it outta yer.

Long beat.

SMUDGE. Are knackerin ent they.

PIDGE. Eh?

SMUDGE. I never bin to one before.

PIDGE. What, like never?

SMUDGE. Na

PIDGE. What about

PUGH. Lucky you

PIDGE. Y'know like…

SMUDGE. What.

PIDGE. Your old man

SMUDGE. Oh. Na.

PIDGE. Yer never went?

SMUDGE. Na

PIDGE. What, yer mum never took yer?

SMUDGE *shakes his head.*

That's a bit fuckin…

SMUDGE *shrugs.*

SMUDGE. I was only two.

PUGH. Three.

SMUDGE. Eh?

PUGH. You were three.

SMUDGE. Was I?

PUGH. Yeah.

SMUDGE. Oh.

SMUDGE counts on his fingers.

Yeah, I was only three.

PIDGE. So what? Two, three, mate, if someone tried to stop me goin…

He shakes his head/puffs out his cheeks.

PUGH. What?

PIDGE. I wouldn't ave it, like, I'd kick right off.

PUGH. At three years old?

PIDGE. Yeah I would / yeah.

PUGH. You're three years old.

PIDGE. So what?

PUGH. You can hardly talk let alone / kick off.

PIDGE. Yeah I'd find a way wouldn't I

PUGH. Alright.

PIDGE. Na I would though

PUGH. You struggle with speaking now

PIDGE. As if, yer fuckin…

Beat.

PUGH. Go on

PIDGE. Latvian.

PUGH. Good one. You've been warned once

SMUDGE. I wouldna wanted to be there anyway I don't think.

PIDGE. Course you would.

SMUDGE. Mmn.

PIDGE. What you talkin about, course you would

SMUDGE. Dunno.

PIDGE. Course you would, why not?

SMUDGE. Horrible ent they?

PUGH. Well. / Yeah.

PIDGE. Yeah they are yeah

SMUDGE. Knew it would be, but.

Beat.

PUGH. Yeah.

PIDGE. Yeah.

PUGH. Did you see his mum?

PIDGE. Yeah.

SMUDGE. Yeah.

Beat.

Fit.

PUGH. I meant the state of her.

SMUDGE. Oh. Yeah.

PUGH. Crying and

SMUDGE. Yeah. That was bad. She is fit though.

PUGH. Well yeah but

SMUDGE. Yeah

PIDGE. Yeah yer would, like

PUGH. Yeah

SMUDGE. Me too

PUGH. But

PIDGE. Yeah

SMUDGE. And his nan.

   Beat.

PUGH. What?

SMUDGE. Bit.

PIDGE. What?!

PUGH. His nan?

SMUDGE. Yeah

PIDGE. You are fuckin jokin?!

SMUDGE. Na / she's

PIDGE. You're not well mate.

SMUDGE. She's got them eyes.

PIDGE. Them eyes? What eyes?

PUGH. She has got eyes

SMUDGE. Them go-to-bed eyes

PIDGE. You fuckin

PUGH. Come, / Smudge.

PIDGE. Titbag.

SMUDGE. What?

PUGH. She's got them *come*-to-bed eyes.

SMUDGE. See, Pughie knows.

PUGH. I'm / not

PIDGE. He's not agreein!

SMUDGE. Pugh?

PUGH. No!

PIDGE. You fuckin…

PUGH. 'Go-to-bed'.

SMUDGE. Whatever, I ain't the only one what thinks she's fit.

PIDGE. Course you are! Frankie's granddad don't even fancy her!

SMUDGE. Yeah but he's like

PUGH. Don't say Frankie's granddad's fit.

SMUDGE. Na, he's like blind en he.

PIDGE. Exactly! Her husband's blind! What does that tell yer?

SMUDGE. What?

PIDGE. That if he coulda seen her he wouldna done it!

SMUDGE. Come on

PUGH. He's right.

PIDGE. She's got a face like a roofer's kneepad mate, I promise yer, like a bag of fuckin spanners.

SMUDGE. Na

PIDGE. Like a bag of spanners up a badger's arsehole.

SMUDGE *shrugs*.

SMUDGE. Well it's my opinion.

PIDGE. Yeah. And it's fuckin wrong.

SMUDGE. Well.

PIDGE. It is though.

SMUDGE. Well

PIDGE. It fuckin is

SMUDGE *shrugs*.

It is.

SMUDGE. My opinion though. So.

PUGH. Good luck to you.

SMUDGE. Cheers.

PUGH. I didn't mean / it.

PIDGE. I tell yer what mate, his granddad don't look like he's got long left so you might still have a chance there

SMUDGE. Oh leave it out.

PIDGE. Leave what out?

SMUDGE. I ain't…

PIDGE. You ain't what?

SMUDGE. Actually gonna

PIDGE. Gonna what?

SMUDGE. Try and do her or

PUGH. Smudge

SMUDGE. I'm sayin I *ain't*!

PIDGE. Yeah but yer just said yer would though

SMUDGE. It's Frankie's nan

PIDGE. But yer just fuckin said

SMUDGE. If she was someone else

PUGH. She's not, so let's leave it shall we?

PIDGE. Na hold up, let's say she is, right, let's just say she's
    some other old bird with a face like a fuckin road map then,
    what, she's gettin a bit of Smudge is she?

    SMUDGE *shrugs*.

SMUDGE. If she wants a bit

PIDGE. I'm gonna have to take you out and get you a bird
    mate, cos that ain't right

SMUDGE. Orses for courses.

PIDGE. You'd be better off if she was a fuckin orse! At least
    she'd have her own teeth!

PUGH. Imagine that.

PIDGE. You imagine it

PUGH. No, not that. Outliving your own grandkid.

    Beat.

PIDGE. Fuckin ell yeah.

Beat.

Kirsty did well, eh? Didn't make a scene or nuffin.

PUGH. Yeah

PIDGE. Good on her, like. Poor cow. Didn't cry or nuffin. Not even when his dad was talkin. I mean I nearly fuckin went then.

Beat.

I thought he might've cracked a joke or summink, dint you? Back at the ouse, just now, lighten the mood a bit

PUGH. I doubt he felt like it mate.

PIDGE. I don't mean a stand-up routine, do I? I just mean a little summink: a mention, a funny story or whatever. People need a laugh dunt they, day like today

PUGH. Do they?

PIDGE. Yeah course they do, what you talkin about? That 'light of our lives' stuff he was doin by the buffet, that ain't gonna do no one any favours is it?

PUGH. Can you hear yourself?

PIDGE. I ain't havin a go, like, I'm just sayin

PUGH. What are you saying?

PIDGE. That people know all that, dunt they? That's why they're there – 's why they're there in the first place cos he's, fuckin… y'know. He's Frankie. They don't need reminding of why they're depressed; what they need is to laugh a bit, innit?

PUGH. Right. You should've told your fish joke.

PIDGE. Yeah I should of, yer right, they'da lapped / it up.

SMUDGE. What's your fish joke?

PUGH. You've heard it.

SMUDGE. I ain't.

PUGH. Trust me

PIDGE. It would've had em rollin

SMUDGE. What / is it?

PUGH. You reckon?

PIDGE. I know it mate, yeah get this:

PUGH. Please don't.

PIDGE. No I ain't doin the joke am I, listen right: my granddad's last year right: me uncles were carryin the box, all the four of em on the four corners, like. Now there's one of em – (*To* SMUDGE.) you've met him as it goes: Divvy Brian.

SMUDGE *looks back blankly.*

Me Uncle Brian – bit fat, sort of bald in the middle.

SMUDGE *shakes his head.*

Divvy Uncle Brian, used to work up Peter Pan's on the burgers, had that funny sort of skin thing on his hands

SMUDGE. Ain't Peter Pan's no more

PIDGE. Na I know that dun I

SMUDGE. Adventure Island

PIDGE. Yeah I know, I can fuckin see it from here

PUGH. No you can't.

PIDGE. Pretty much.

PUGH. With your good eye?

PIDGE. Fuck off

PUGH. You should try and get a job there; they'd love a real pirate

PIDGE. I'm tryina tell a fuckin story here, d'yer mind?

PUGH. Get on with it then!

PIDGE. I'm tryin en I?! Right, right me Uncle Brian, who's a div, who used to work up Peter Pan's when it was still Peter Pan's, who Smudge has met

SMUDGE. Hang on, is he the one what looks like a fat Paul Daniels?

PIDGE. Yes!

SMUDGE. I have met him.

PIDGE. I know you have!

SMUDGE. Why d'you reckon they changed it? I liked it better as Peter Pan's.

PIDGE. You don't remember it

SMUDGE. I do

PIDGE. We was only just born

SMUDGE. But I remember though

PIDGE. Bull/shit

PUGH. What's wrong with Adventure Island?

SMUDGE *shrugs*.

SMUDGE. Not much adventure.

Beat.

PUGH. Fair point

SMUDGE. So why d'you reckon they changed it?

PUGH. I think it got bought out

PIDGE. Na it never

PUGH. Yeah it did.

PIDGE. Na it never, they was sued by Disney

Beat.

PUGH. What did you just say?

PIDGE. Walt Disney sued em and that for usin the name

PUGH. What are you talking about?

PIDGE. That's why they had to change it / to whassit

PUGH. Walt Disney's been dead since about nineteen-fifty

PIDGE. Well not him then, his kids, or like the firm, or whatever

PUGH. He didn't invent Peter Pan

PIDGE. Course he did

PUGH. No he didn't, it was already a book

PIDGE. Who by?

PUGH. I don't know

PIDGE. Yeah exactly

PUGH. It's not Walt Disney

PIDGE. Yeah it is.

PUGH. It's not, Pidge!

PIDGE. Look it up then

PUGH. I'm not looking it up

PIDGE. Cos yer know I'm right

PUGH. No you're not

PIDGE. Look it up then

PUGH. No, we said no phones

PIDGE. I'm looking it up

PUGH. No phones

PIDGE. Then agree I'm right.

PUGH. But you're not

PIDGE. But I am though

PUGH. Whatever

SMUDGE. It's Barry someone

PIDGE. What?

SMUDGE. It's Barry someone what writ *Peter Pan*

PUGH. How do you know?

SMUDGE *shrugs*.

SMUDGE. Some things you know.

PIDGE. It's Barry Disney then

PUGH. Oh stop it

PIDGE. You fuckin stop it, I'm tellin yer summink here, you might learn

PUGH. I doubt it

PIDGE. Right, shut up, so he's stepped in dogshit outside the church, right, and don't know he's done it

SMUDGE. Who?

PIDGE. Divvy Brian, my uncle – fuck me it's hard work.

SMUDGE. Go on.

PIDGE. Right he's stepped in dogshit and it's just as they're pickin him up, me granddad, and he's on one of the back corners of the coffin, Brian, so no one's noticed… well: he's traipsed it all the way down through the church, en e? Right up to the front to the, whassit, where they put im down and / that

PUGH. The altar.

PIDGE. The what?

PUGH. The altar.

PIDGE. Na the thing, the – anyway he's left dogshit all the way up the aisle of the church, yer shoulda seen it, great big fuckin smears of it, stunk an all – I mean it proper, properly hummed, like. And my mum's there, sittin there front row, dressed in black, pack of tissues and that, she gets a whiff, turns around and sees this fuckin… brown and yellow fuckin trail comin from the door all the way up to Divvy Brian standin there in his suit and his backwards face like a fat Paul Daniels with it all over his shoe. Well, she thought it was hilarious me mum. Couldn't stop herself laughing. Wettin herself, she couldn't *breathe* she was laughing so hard, and then she farted and set everyone else off.

SMUDGE *is laughing/grinning*.

Yer see?

PUGH. What?

PIDGE. Point proved.

PUGH. There was a point to that?

PIDGE. Yeah I'm just sayin: people wanna cry, they'll laugh at anything.

Beat.

PUGH. Did that happen?

PIDGE. What?

PUGH. Did that / happen?

PIDGE. Yeah, I just told yer didn't I? Ask my mum.

PUGH. Alright.

PIDGE. Go on then

PUGH. I will yeah

PIDGE. Go on

PUGH. Yeah I will

PIDGE. Go on then, cos she'll tell yer

PUGH. Alright

PIDGE. 'Did that happen' yer cheeky fuck.

SMUDGE. They always that long? The things.

PUGH. The

PIDGE. Yeah it did go on a bit, like

PUGH. Fuck me

PIDGE. What? It's the truth / ennit.

SMUDGE. I ain't sayin I was bored, I just never bin, so

PUGH. It 'went on a bit'?

PIDGE. Yeah come on, they didn't have to do every bit of that song, did they, for a start, the fuckin hymn thing

SMUDGE. I just wondered

PIDGE. Alright, we get it: he's basically got *everything* in his hands then en e?

PUGH. Unbelievable

PIDGE. Job done. In his massive fuckin great big hands.

SMUDGE. Thought they might've made it longer for all the people

PIDGE. It was ten minutes that one song!

SMUDGE. Know what I mean?

PIDGE. I don't care what you say, that's / too much

PUGH. Alright

SMUDGE. Like they judge it on how many's there, or summink.

PUGH. What are you saying Smudge?

SMUDGE. Cos more people wanna come and speak, do they make it longer?

PUGH. I don't think so mate

SMUDGE. Oh

PUGH. I think it's just booked by the hour

PIDGE. There was about fifty fuckers in there I'd never even seen before in me life, where did they all come from?

PUGH. They probably just go to the church

PIDGE. And what about Lee Blackshot and that lot in the corner, who the fuck invited them? Frankie never even liked em

SMUDGE. They joined the Facebook thing

PIDGE. Who set that up?

SMUDGE. I did. His mum said.

PIDGE. Yer shoulda put a lock on it or summink

PUGH. What for? If they wanted to pay their respects

PIDGE. Respects my arse, they just wanted to hang about and put on a fuckin suit

SMUDGE. Dint you just nick him?

PUGH. Yeah. Well I didn't, but he was in court for beating up his girlfriend.

PIDGE. Blackshot?

PUGH. Yeah. Same suit.

PIDGE. See they're scumbags, shouldna bin there, that lot

PUGH. They were alright today.

PIDGE. Yeah tell that to his bird.

PUGH. She had an eye like yours

PIDGE. Fuck off

SMUDGE. What's that?

PIDGE. What's what?

SMUDGE. You farted?

PIDGE. Yeah. Yer lucky that's all I've done mate

PUGH. Give it a rest

PIDGE. I gotta drop the kids off at the pool though en I. Take Mr and Mrs Brown and the kids to the seaside

PUGH. Can you stop talking about shit

PIDGE. It's alright for you, I can feel it brewing, it's a big one

SMUDGE. Why don't you go?

PUGH. Stay there.

PIDGE. That's why

PUGH. She'll be here in a minute.

PIDGE. What's the hold-up?

PUGH. I dunno.

PIDGE. What time did she say?

PUGH. I don't / know.

PIDGE. Cos I'm runnin out of beer here an all.

PUGH. And is that more important?

PIDGE. I ain't sayin that am I? But I gotta have a beer to be able to cheers him when we're, whassit, lettin the balloons go or whatever.

SMUDGE. I still don't get it.

PIDGE. We can't sit here and do it / empty-handed.

PUGH. What don't you get?

SMUDGE. Balloons. What have balloons got to do with anyfin?

PUGH. It's. I don't know. Symbolic.

SMUDGE. What of?

PUGH. I don't. His soul?

Beat.

Ask Kirsty.

SMUDGE. Alright.

Beat.

He dint really like balloons though did he? The squeak they make.

Beat.

The chimes of an ice-cream van from off. SMUDGE *looks toward the sound.*

Beat.

Anyone want an ice cream?

PUGH. No

PIDGE. You don't do yer?

SMUDGE. Na

PIDGE. I was gunna say

SMUDGE. Yeah...

Beat.

SMUDGE *looks off longingly towards the chimes again.*

Beat.

Shall we play a game?

PIDGE. No.

SMUDGE. Alright.

Long beat.

I saw a midget yesterday.

Long beat.

I spy with my little eye something beginning / with

PIDGE. Fuck off.

SMUDGE. Why?

PIDGE. I spy?

A slight smile from PUGH *re:* PIDGE*'s eyepatch. The penny drops for* SMUDGE.

SMUDGE. Oh na, I weren't…

PIDGE. Oh na.

SMUDGE. I weren't. Just thought.

PIDGE. Thought what?

SMUDGE. Dunno.

PIDGE. 'Dunno'.

SMUDGE. Break the silence.

PIDGE. Alright, well don't; leave it whole.

SMUDGE. Do what?

PIDGE. Leave it in one piece.

SMUDGE. The…?

PIDGE. The silence yeah, you break it you buy it.

SMUDGE. Eh?

PIDGE. That's a fiver.

SMUDGE. What is?

PIDGE. You owe me a fiver.

SMUDGE. What for?

PIDGE. For the silence.

PUGH. Shut up. Ignore him.

SMUDGE. I don't get it.

PUGH. He's talking shit again, that's why.

PIDGE. Who is?

PUGH. You are! It's relentless!

PIDGE. Fuck you.

PUGH. You wish.

PIDGE. *You* wish. Mate if I was gonna go bent I could do better than you.

PUGH. You reckon?

PIDGE. I know it mate.

PUGH. Like who?

PIDGE. What?

PUGH. Who?

   PIDGE *thinks for a beat.*

PIDGE. I ain't fuckin. Whoever, I ain't sittin here thinkin about blokes.

PUGH. That'll make a change.

PIDGE. Shut up.

PUGH. I'm trying to! You keep on talking!

   Long beat.

SMUDGE. Eh?

PIDGE. What?

SMUDGE. What'd you say?

PIDGE. When?

SMUDGE. Just now.

PIDGE. Nuffin.

SMUDGE. Oh.

Beat.

Thought you said summink.

PIDGE. Na. That'll just be the voices in yer head.

Long beat.

PUGH. Sod this.

PUGH takes a fresh pack of cigarettes from his inside pocket and starts unwrapping the cellophane.

PIDGE. Hang about, what are they?

PUGH. Cigarettes, Pidge.

PIDGE. I can see, I know they're fuckin – you're a cunt intcher? What I mean is, is I thought you'd given up?

PUGH. I have.

He puts a fag in his mouth and offers the box to PIDGE – *who also takes one.*

PIDGE. Looks like it.

PUGH. Jenna asks: I have.

SMUDGE. Can I have one?

PUGH. No.

PIDGE. No.

SMUDGE. Why not?

PUGH. You don't smoke.

SMUDGE. Nor do you, you've given up.

PUGH. Looks like it.

SMUDGE. Go on, please.

PUGH. No, Smudge.

SMUDGE. Why not?

PUGH. Smoking kills.

SMUDGE. One won't.

PUGH. You never know. And I could do with you sticking about.

Beat.

SMUDGE. Yeah

PUGH. You got a light?

PIDGE. Yeah I have as it goes, a new one. Zippo.

PUGH. Go on then.

PIDGE. It's in me coat.

PUGH. Where's your coat?

PIDGE. At the ouse.

PUGH. Then why'd you say you had a / light

PIDGE. Cos I have, en I? I have *got* a light

PUGH. A mile away.

PIDGE. That ain't a mile

PUGH. Whatever it is

PIDGE. I've still got one.

PUGH. Congratulations. I've got a blowtorch in my shed

SMUDGE. Have / yer?

PUGH. Can't light my fag with that either, can I?

PIDGE. I'm just sayin.

PUGH. What are you saying?

PIDGE. That I've got a light!

PUGH. But you haven't, Pidge!

PIDGE. But I fuckin have though!

PUGH. Can you light it?

PIDGE. What?

PUGH. Can you light my fag?

PIDGE. What, now?

PUGH. Yes now!

PIDGE. Well, na, but

PUGH. Right. So please. Shut up.

SMUDGE. How comes you've got a blowtorch?

Beat.

PUGH. What?

SMUDGE. Have you been welding?

PUGH. Yeah I've been welding.

SMUDGE. Have yer?

PUGH. No! Why would I have been welding?

SMUDGE. Dunno.

PUGH. I haven't.

SMUDGE. So why you got a blowtorch / in yer

PUGH. I haven't, Smudge.

SMUDGE. You said.

PUGH. I haven't got a blowtorch.

SMUDGE. Oh.

PUGH. I haven't even got a shed.

SMUDGE. Oh yeah.

PUGH. It was a figure of speech.

SMUDGE. Oh right. I ain't heard it before.

Beat.

PIDGE. Was you dropped on your head as a kid or summink?

SMUDGE. I was as it goes.

PIDGE. You what?

SMUDGE. Yeah my mum fell off a bus.

PUGH. And dropped you on your head?

SMUDGE. On the pavement, yeah. Parently I bounced like a football.

SMUDGE *seems somehow proud of this.*

Beat.

PIDGE. Well that explains that then.

PUGH. What's your excuse?

PIDGE. Your mum.

PUGH. Brilliant.

PIDGE. Yer gonna get it then or what?

PUGH. Get what?

PIDGE. My lighter.

PUGH. No!

PIDGE. Suit yourself.

PUGH. You get it!

PIDGE. Fuck off, it's miles away

PUGH. You just / said

PIDGE. And anyway, e's got one, en e. Oi Dan

PUGH. Leave him.

PIDGE. Dan!

PUGH. Pidge. Forget / it.

PIDGE. Dan!

PUGH. Pigeon.

PIDGE. Oi, Gay Boy!

DAN *looks up as if woken from a dream.* PIDGE *grins.*

Yer know yer name then.

DAN....

PUGH. You got a light?

DAN *fishes it out of his pocket.*

Cheers.

He throws it up to PUGH *who lights his own cigarette and then* PIDGE*'s. Looks back down to* DAN, *but he's gone back to staring out over the sea.*

PUGH *pockets the lighter.*

PIDGE *drags on his cigarette and makes a hacking noise at the taste.*

PIDGE. Fuckin Nora!

PUGH. 'Fucking Nora'?

PIDGE. These are fuckin

PUGH. Yeah.

PIDGE *inspects the writing on the paper.*

PIDGE. Rothmans?

PUGH. Making up for lost time.

PIDGE. Yeah no shit, it's like I'm chewin on a cigar.

PUGH. I'll smoke it if you don't want it

PIDGE. Na I'll smoke it, like

PUGH. Stop whinging then

SMUDGE. I'll smoke it.

PUGH. No

PIDGE. No you won't, yer fuckin ponce.

SMUDGE. Ain't even yours!

PIDGE. Yeah it is now though.

SMUDGE. Sod yer then.

SMUDGE fishes a sausage roll out of his pocket and starts eating it.

Beat.

PIDGE. You've gotta be fuckin jokin?

SMUDGE. What?

PIDGE. Why have you got sausage rolls in your pocket?

SMUDGE. Took one in case.

PIDGE. In case of what?

SMUDGE. Case I got hungry.

PIDGE. And hold up, hang about, what, you're hungry now are yer?

SMUDGE shrugs.

SMUDGE. Bit.

PIDGE. I've just watched you eat five Scotch eggs!

SMUDGE. When?

PIDGE. When?!

SMUDGE. That was ages ago

PUGH. What happened to your diet?

PIDGE. Five Scotch eggs, / Pugh

SMUDGE. It was only four

PIDGE. Not the little ones, like, not them little ones with the fuckin like the whassit, little egg-mayonnaisey crumble shit in – five whole Scotch eggs.

SMUDGE. Four

PUGH. That's

PIDGE. Five

PUGH. How's that being on a diet?

SMUDGE. I know but

PIDGE. And now sausage rolls out / yer pocket.

SMUDGE. I know

PUGH. Smudge.

SMUDGE. It's a buffet ennit? They want it eaten.

PIDGE. Oh yeah na, 's good of yer / really

SMUDGE. Leave it out

PIDGE. Mate there's starvin Africans down the A127 woulda loved that sausage roll

SMUDGE. I'll start the diet again tomorrow

PIDGE. Course you will yeah

SMUDGE. I will. But if it's alright wiv you I've had a bit of a shit day, so.

Beat.

PIDGE. Yeah alright.

PUGH. Yeah sorry.

Beat.

PIDGE. Sorry.

Beat.

But five Scotch / eggs

SMUDGE. Oh!

SMUDGE *tosses the sausage roll onto the sand.*

Beat.

PIDGE. Well that's a waste.

SMUDGE. Where is she? We bin here ages.

PUGH. Yeah. Alright I'll ring her.

PIDGE. You had her number all this time?

PUGH. Yeah course I have.

PIDGE. Then why ain't you phoned her already?!

PUGH. Because we said / no phones

SMUDGE. No phones

PIDGE. Fuck that I bin touchin cloth for half hour – you tell her I need a shit

PUGH. Yeah I'll do that

PIDGE. And get us a beer while yer up

PUGH. I'm not going anywhere

PIDGE. Go on

PUGH. No Pidge.

PIDGE. Go on

PUGH. You'll have to wait

PIDGE. There's only backwash left in here

PUGH. Well tough.

PIDGE. You want me to send Frankie's soul into the air with a mouthful of backwash?

PUGH. No

PIDGE. Well / then

PUGH. I want you to stop showing off and have a bit of respect.

Beat.

PIDGE. What?

PUGH. Back in a minute.

PIDGE....

> PUGH *walks off to make the call.*

> That was a bit fuckin strong weren't it?

> *Beat.*

SMUDGE. D'you want a bit of my beer?

PIDGE. Na yer alright.

SMUDGE. You sure?

PIDGE. Yeah yer fine.

Beat.

(Cunt.) Not you.

SMUDGE. Alright.

PIDGE. You gonna join us or what?

Beat.

Oi you, Daniel-son, you gonna join us today or what? Or you gonna camp out on yer own all day down there like a cunt?

DAN....

PIDGE. What's that face?

DAN. I'm

PIDGE. What?

DAN. I'm here, aren't I?

PIDGE. Yeah just about. I ain't heard a peep outta yer yet.

Beat.

DAN. I don't. Really know what to say.

PIDGE. Fuck me, there's a first. Can't normally shut you up.

DAN *feigns a smile.*

Beat.

I was surprised you never done a readin as it appens.

Beat.

Danny Boy.

DAN. Yeah

PIDGE. I said I thought you woulda done us a reading

DAN. No

PIDGE. How comes? The rest of us did.

DAN. I'm just not. Much good in church.

PIDGE. Na?

DAN. No. Not really.

PIDGE. Ah.

>*Beat.*

>But you was there.

DAN....

PIDGE. You was there, in the church.

DAN. Yeah of course I. So were you. So was everyone else

PIDGE. Yeah I'm a Christian

DAN. Right

SMUDGE. I'm not

PIDGE. I was christened in that church

SMUDGE. Me too

DAN. Well there you go.

PIDGE. But you weren't.

DAN. No.

PIDGE. So you're no good in churches.

DAN. No.

PIDGE. So...

DAN. What? I was hardly going to miss it was I?

PIDGE. Just checkin.

DAN. What?

PIDGE. Just checkin. Cos yer nearly did, didn't yer?

DAN....

PIDGE. That's why you was sittin up the back on yer tod weren't it?

DAN. Why?

PIDGE. Cos yer got there late.

DAN. I wasn't late.

PIDGE. Well yer weren't early was yer?

DAN. And I wasn't late, so / I was

PIDGE. You only beat Frankie in by about a minute

DAN. So I was on time.

Beat.

PIDGE. Lucky us, eh?

DAN. What?

PIDGE. What's the matter you goin deaf?

DAN. What is the matter with you?

Just then, PUGH *returns.*

PUGH. They haven't delivered.

Beat.

PIDGE. You what?

PUGH. They haven't delivered

PIDGE. Yer fuckin / jokin?

SMUDGE. Really?

PIDGE. Yer jokin?

PUGH. No.

PIDGE. What a bunch of

PUGH. Yeah

SMUDGE. That's

PUGH. Yeah. It is.

DAN. So

PIDGE. Cunts

DAN. What now?

PUGH. We wait some more. Hello, by the way.

PIDGE. We wait for what?

PUGH. They're getting them elsewhere.

SMUDGE. Who is?

PIDGE. So they ain't even fuckin replaced em?

PUGH. No.

PIDGE. What a fuckin

PUGH. Not open Mondays, apparently.

DAN. Then how were they delivering in the first place?

PUGH. They weren't, I spose.

PIDGE. Now *that* is symbolic.

SMUDGE. Who's gettin / em?

PIDGE. Sym-bollocks.

PUGH. Kirsty. They're driving there now she said.

SMUDGE. Who's they?

DAN. What, Kirsty's driving?

PUGH. I doubt it.

PIDGE. Well she can't now can / she

SMUDGE. So who's she with?

PUGH. I don't

SMUDGE. That Greg bloke?

PUGH. Who?

SMUDGE. That bloke from her work?

PUGH. Don't know, I didn't ask.

PIDGE. See he's another one right; what's he doin here?

DAN. Is he sober?

PIDGE. I bet Frank dint know him from Adam

DAN. Has anyone seen him drink?

PUGH. Who?

DAN. This Greg. If he's the one driving. Has he had a drink today?

Beat.

PUGH. I'll ring her back

SMUDGE. Na I'll do it, I'll go, I'll do it.

PUGH. Yeah?

SMUDGE. What's her number?

SMUDGE *gets up, a bit too keen.*

PUGH. Here.

SMUDGE. Want to talk to her anyway.

PUGH. Alright.

PUGH *taps his phone.*

It's ringing.

SMUDGE. Two minutes.

SMUDGE *takes* PUGH's *phone and goes off.*

Beat.

PUGH. That was weird.

PIDGE. Well yer know what it is.

PUGH. What is it?

PIDGE. He fancies her.

PUGH. What?

PIDGE. He does, I'm tellin / yer.

PUGH. Kirsty? Shut up. It's Kirsty.

PIDGE. Yeah and it's Smudge

PUGH. What does that mean?

PIDGE. He fancies everyone.

PUGH. Coming from you!

PIDGE. Just cos I fuck a lot of birds mate don't mean I fancy em

DAN. Dripping with class.

PIDGE. Dripping with gash mate – and don't you forget it

PUGH. You're back with us then.

DAN. Who me?

PUGH. Now I mean. Not

DAN. Right. Yeah

PUGH. Today. Here

DAN. Yeah.

PUGH. Not. When's it booked?

DAN. What?

PUGH. The new flight.

DAN. Oh. It's not. As yet.

   Beat.

PUGH. No?

DAN. No.

PUGH. So you about for a bit?

DAN. Maybe.

PIDGE. You about next Monday then?

DAN. Why? What's happening Monday?

PIDGE. 'What's happening Monday'.

   Beat.

DAN. What…

PIDGE. Yeah.

PUGH. What? No.

PIDGE. What d'you mean 'no'?

PUGH. No. I mean

DAN. No; that's

PUGH. That's it

PIDGE. Fuck off.

Beat.

Why?

DAN. 'Why?'

PIDGE. Is there an echo?

PUGH. Of course that's it.

PIDGE. Why is it?

PUGH. We can't carry on with it now.

PIDGE. Yeah course we can

PUGH. What are you talking about? We can't play five-a-side with just three of us anyway

PIDGE. It's still four till he fucks off ennit

PUGH. It's five-a-side

PIDGE. Well we'll find people, wunt we

PUGH. I don't wanna just.

PIDGE. What.

PUGH. Plug gaps.

PIDGE. Why not? We gotta carry on ent we? For Frankie, like. And he's shit anyway.

PUGH. It's not about that, is it?

DAN. And I'm not.

PIDGE. Well you are

DAN. No I'm / not

PIDGE. You are though

DAN. I'm better than you!

PIDGE. You fuckin wish you was!

PUGH. It's not about

DAN. I am.

PIDGE. As if mate!

PUGH. It's not about

PIDGE. As if yer better than me! Who scored their fuckin penalty?

DAN. Here we go.

PIDGE. Who scored their penalty?

PUGH. Oh / for f

DAN. We were seventeen!

PIDGE. Who scored their penalty?!

DAN. Yes alright! I missed a penalty!

PIDGE. Not *a* penalty mate

DAN. Alright, yes!

PIDGE. *The* penalty.

DAN. Let it go!

PIDGE. No chance.

DAN. What do you think would have happened if we'd won?

PIDGE. Yeah exactly, who fuckin knows?

DAN. You think you'd be playing for Arsenal now?

PIDGE. Na

DAN. No

PIDGE. West Ham, QPR

DAN. Of course you would.

PIDGE. I fuckin would mate, it's National Schools, there'da been scouts everywhere at the final.

DAN. And they wouldn't have looked at you twice!

PIDGE. They'da picked me fore they picked you I fuckin tell yer that much.

DAN. If you say so

PIDGE. Yeah course they would

DAN. Right I'm bored now

PIDGE. Na, don't try and mug me off

PUGH. Alright…

DAN. I'm not *trying* to do anything, / Pidge.

PUGH. Girls.

PIDGE. What about him, then?

DAN. Who?

PUGH. What about me?

PIDGE. He coulda done it, like

PUGH. Leave it now

PIDGE. He coulda gone pro, bin someone could Pugh

PUGH. Pidge

PIDGE. And instead he's a fuckin no one like the rest of us

PUGH. Oi!

DAN. Speak for yourself.

PIDGE. It's true ennit?

PUGH. No!

DAN. No

PIDGE. Na?

PUGH. No. Thanks.

PIDGE. Who are *you* then?

PUGH. What?

PIDGE. Who knows *your* name?

PUGH. No one

PIDGE. Na exactly

PUGH. But that's

PIDGE. And what about you, hotshot? What are you to the world?

DAN....

PIDGE. Eh? Cept another city suit. Eh? Who's gonna remember you when yer dead?

DAN. You are.

PIDGE. Yeah, for fuckin up me chances

DAN. Right

PUGH. Look

DAN. Listen to me

PUGH. There's more important / things.

DAN. Listen:

PIDGE. Yeah?

DAN. I say this as a mate: you're shit at football, Pidge.

PIDGE. Fuck you

DAN. You never would've made it, regardless

PUGH. Dan, come / on

PIDGE. What the fuck do you know?

PUGH. Lads

DAN. I know plenty

PIDGE. Who scored their penalty?

DAN. Right I give / up.

PUGH. It was years ago.

DAN. Thank you.

PUGH. There are more important things.

PIDGE. Like what?

Just then, SMUDGE *returns.*

SMUDGE. 'S alright, she's wiv her dad.

PUGH. Who, Kirsty?

PIDGE. Pugh.

SMUDGE. Yeah the bloke's gone home, so.

PUGH. So…?

SMUDGE. Oh nuffin. Na. Gone home, that's all.

DAN. Who?

SMUDGE. That Greg.

   SMUDGE *hands* PUGH *his phone back*

DAN. So her dad's driving?

SMUDGE. Yeah

DAN. Okay, good

PIDGE. Pugh

SMUDGE. Yeah 's what I meant

PIDGE. Tell me.

PUGH. What?

PIDGE. What's more important than that?

SMUDGE. Than what?

PIDGE. Than bein someone.

   Beat.

PUGH. I'm gonna ask Jenna to marry me.

   Beat.

PIDGE. Fuck me.

SMUDGE. What, / really?

PIDGE. Fuck. Me.

PUGH. Yeah

PIDGE. Mate

DAN. Congratulations

PUGH. I haven't asked her yet

PIDGE. Mate

PUGH. She might say no

PIDGE. If she's got any fuckin sense / yeah

PUGH. Oh d'you know what

SMUDGE. You thought about it?

PUGH. Yeah. I haven't just made it up.

SMUDGE. Na I mean / how you're gonna

PIDGE. *Have* you thought about it?

PUGH. Course I have

DAN. Of course he has

PIDGE. That's yer life mate

PUGH. I know

PIDGE. The fuckin rest o yer life

PUGH. Yeah I know

PIDGE. Yer still young. From the forehead down.

PUGH. Fuck off

SMUDGE. My parents met

PUGH. Look I love her. / So

PIDGE. Queer.

PUGH. I've got the job, I've got the house

PIDGE. Yer got the mortgage yer mean

SMUDGE. My parents / were

PUGH. I want to have kids

PIDGE. Yeah like one day yeah, not now

SMUDGE. They were only

PUGH. Soon

PIDGE. Leave it out!

SMUDGE. They were only eleven.

Beat.

PIDGE. You what?

SMUDGE. My mum and dad.

PIDGE. When they got married?

SMUDGE. Na, when they met.

PIDGE. So what's that got to do wiv anyfin?

Beat.

SMUDGE. Dunno.

PUGH. Look. I went to see the car. At the nick.

DAN. You…?

PUGH. While they were doing the thing. The inquest. It's still there, I / suppose.

SMUDGE. You went and see it?

PUGH. Yeah

DAN. Why?

PUGH. I knew the blokes who'd been called out

PIDGE. Did yer?

PUGH. It didn't feel right they'd seen it and not me.

SMUDGE. Was he…?

PUGH. Was who what?

SMUDGE. Frankie. Was he still

PUGH. No. This was much. Days later.

SMUDGE. Oh.

PUGH. But.

Beat.

DAN. What?

PUGH. They don't clean them out before they scrap em. So.

Beat.

They tried to give me his effects bag to give to his mum. His watch was in it.

Beat.

And I thought to myself. Yeah. What am I waiting for? Jenna's been put there, this close to me on the planet. Give it a bash.

PIDGE. You're gonna marry her cos of geography?

PUGH. I wouldn't expect you to understand

SMUDGE. You farted again?

PIDGE. Yeah I have / yeah

SMUDGE. It's really bad

PIDGE. Yeah it's gonna be, en it? I'm bein denied my human right to shit.

DAN. So when will you do it? Not you

PUGH. Next week I think. I've booked us into a Gordon Ramsay

SMUDGE. Nice

PIDGE. Fuck me it gets worse

PUGH. Oh someone turn him off

PIDGE. He's a cunt though en e, Ramsay.

PUGH. Why is he?

DAN. He speaks very highly of you.

PIDGE. Pretends to be Scottish dun he, the cunt.

SMUDGE. Does he?

PIDGE. In charity matches an that

DAN. He is.

SMUDGE. What, Scottish?

DAN. Yeah

SMUDGE. Is he?

PIDGE. Yeah he sounds it.

DAN. He is.

PIDGE. Then why's he talk like that then, eh? He don't sound Scottish to me.

PUGH. You don't sound like a pirate, but

He indicates his eyepatch. The chimes of the ice-cream van sound again. Only SMUDGE *responds, looking off.*

PIDGE. Shut up, I've fuckin told yer, about that.

PUGH. Alright don't rape and pillage me.

PIDGE. I coulda gone blind yer fuckin

PUGH. Alright.

PIDGE. Ask the doctor!

PUGH. I'll do that / yeah

PIDGE. He said a couple of inches left or right

PUGH. A couple of inches?

PIDGE. A couple of millimetres

PUGH. A couple of *inches* and it wouldn't have hit you

PIDGE. A couple of millimetres he said and I coulda gone blind

PUGH. Just as well you didn't

PIDGE. Exactly

PUGH. You'd be out of the game.

PIDGE. Exactly. What game?

PUGH. Smudge?

SMUDGE. What

PUGH. You doing the honours?

SMUDGE. Of what?

PUGH. I spy.

PIDGE. Fuck off.

PUGH. I'll go then shall I? I spy with my little / eye

PIDGE. Prick.

PUGH. I spy with my little prick, something beginning with 'S'.

PIDGE. No one's gonna play

SMUDGE. Sea.

PUGH. No 'S'.

SMUDGE. Na sea.

DAN. That's a river.

SMUDGE. Is it?

DAN. Yeah it's the Thames

SMUDGE. Oh.

DAN. You've lived here all your / life

SMUDGE. Sand then

PUGH. No

SMUDGE. Stones

PUGH. No

SMUDGE. Sun?

PIDGE. What?

PUGH. No

PIDGE. You can't even see / the sun

PUGH. Shut up

DAN. Shingle.

PUGH. No

SMUDGE. Sky

PUGH. No

PIDGE. Smudge.

SMUDGE. What?

PIDGE. No, you; Smudge

PUGH. You're not playing.

SMUDGE. Me.

PUGH. No

PIDGE. Shells, then

PUGH. You're not playing.

SMUDGE. Is it shells?

PUGH. No

PIDGE. What is it then?

PUGH. Shush.

PIDGE. What?

PUGH. Keep out.

PIDGE. Tell me.

PUGH. No.

PIDGE. What is it?

PUGH. You're not playing.

PIDGE. You're a dick.

PUGH. Give up?

SMUDGE. Na.

PIDGE *takes his phone out of his pocket and begins fiddling with it.*

PUGH. Oi, put that away.

PIDGE. No I'm / doing summink

SMUDGE. (Smmer, Sper…)

PUGH. Then look up Peter Pan.

PIDGE. I already know who done it so I don't need to look it up, do I?

PUGH. It's not Walt / Disney!

SMUDGE. (Spler... Ster...)

DAN. It's JM Barrie.

PUGH. What?

DAN. JM Barrie wrote *Peter Pan*.

PUGH. Yeah?

DAN. Seems. Apt.

PIDGE. What?

DAN. Peter Pan. The boy who never grew up.

PIDGE. Why's that 'seem apt'?

SMUDGE. Sssssssssssssssssssssssssss / ssssssssssssssssss...

PIDGE. You got a puncture?

SMUDGE. Shoes!

PUGH. No.

SMUDGE. Oh.

PUGH. You were right about Peter Pan Smudge

SMUDGE. Yeah?

PUGH. Barry someone. Sort of.

SMUDGE. Told ya.

PIDGE. Someone Barrie not Barry someone.

PUGH. Not Disney is it?

PIDGE. Who fuckin cares anyway?

SMUDGE. Is it shirts?

PUGH. What?

SMUDGE. Shirts

PUGH. No

SMUDGE. Suits?

PUGH. No

PIDGE. Shit?

PUGH. Closer.

PIDGE. You might see it soon if she don't / hurry up.

PUGH. You're still not playing.

SMUDGE. Ships. Shops.

PIDGE. Where's there shops you can see?!

PUGH. Getting colder.

DAN. It is.

PUGH. What was that?

DAN. It is a bit. Getting colder. Did she say how long she'd be?

PUGH. Not to me

DAN. Smudge?

SMUDGE. Na

PIDGE. Here right, have a look at this

PUGH. No more phones

PIDGE. Look, here.

PUGH. What is it?

PIDGE. Have a look.

He gives PUGH *his phone to show him what he's been doing.*

Beat.

PUGH. *Football Focus*?

PIDGE. Yeah.

PUGH. Why are you showing me

PIDGE. It's the one wiv Gary Speed on.

PUGH. What…

PIDGE. Yeah, the last one, before he / went and

DAN. Why have you got that on your phone?

PIDGE. Na I ain't have I, it's on whassit

SMUDGE. YouTube.

PIDGE. YouTube, yeah.

DAN. Why?

PIDGE. Why? So people can watch it.

DAN. Well yeah. / But why?

PUGH. Have it back.

SMUDGE. Can I have a look?

PIDGE. Go on, yeah.

PUGH. Don't bother, Smudge

He passes the phone to SMUDGE.

DAN. Why have you got that up?

PIDGE. Cos it's weird ennit

DAN. Yeah. It is

PIDGE. One minute he's all like laughing and that

DAN. It's morbid

PIDGE. And then he goes home and tops himself

PUGH. Alright!

PIDGE. Yer know what I mean though? They'da never have
known it was comin.

PUGH. So?

They look at each other.

Beat.

No.

PIDGE. Na?

PUGH. No!

DAN. No!

PIDGE. Na.

PUGH. No, *no* / Pidge.

PIDGE. I'm sayin no en I?

PUGH. But you're thinking 'yes'

PIDGE. How am I?

PUGH. You are

PIDGE. You a fuckin mind-reader / now?

DAN. Why say, why would you say something like that?

PIDGE. Cos other people are sayin ent they, so

PUGH. Who are?

PIDGE. People, I dunno.

DAN. What people?

PIDGE. I don't fuckin – people, like, Facebook people – them other cunts – they bin sayin stuff ent they, you know they have. I'm just seein where we all stand on it.

PUGH. We don't.

PIDGE. We don't what?

PUGH. Stand on it. Anywhere

DAN. No

PUGH. At all. So you can leave it

PIDGE. Alright then, good, I'm just seein, en I?

PUGH. Now you know.

PIDGE. Alright then

DAN. Yeah

PIDGE. What about you?

PUGH. Pidge…

SMUDGE. Eh?

PIDGE. What. I'm askin

PUGH. Leave it alone

PIDGE. What d'you reckon on it?

SMUDGE. What?

PIDGE. What I just said.

SMUDGE. What's that?

DAN. Pigeon.

PIDGE. What I just asked Pugh.

SMUDGE. Oh I dunno I was watching / Gary Speed.

DAN. Forget it, Smudge. Ignore him.

PIDGE. Frankie

PUGH. Pidge!

SMUDGE. What about / him?

PIDGE. Look I've asked you, you've had your say, I wanna know what Smudge thinks

SMUDGE. What about?!

PIDGE. Was it an accident? Frankie. Or was it, like

DAN. It was an accident.

SMUDGE. I dunno.

PUGH. What?

SMUDGE *shrugs*.

DAN. It was an accident.

PUGH. Of course it was an accident

PIDGE. Smudge?

PUGH. I'll throw you off this wall, you carry on.

PIDGE. Yeah you can try.

DAN. There's no. He had no reason / to

PUGH. Why would he?

PIDGE. Smudge?

SMUDGE. Dunno

DAN. Because he didn't

SMUDGE. I just been thinkin

PIDGE. See?

PUGH. Why though?

PIDGE. I told yer people been sayin

DAN. He's not – you haven't said anything?

SMUDGE. Na

DAN. Good

PUGH. Good

SMUDGE. I just been thinkin

PIDGE. Same thing ennit

DAN. How is that the same?

PIDGE. Cos it is; cos it means other people have been thinkin it as well, dunnit? Not everyone's just gone: 'oh what a shame, what a tragic fuckin accident'

DAN. That's what it is

PIDGE. Or maybe it ain't though

PUGH. Bollocks.

DAN. Why? Because Smudge has been 'thinking about it'? Well that's hardly concrete proof

PIDGE. Yeah I ain't talkin about proof, am I? I'm talkin about what we all think

PUGH. I just told you

DAN. Look I'm not being funny mate

PIDGE. Yer never are, / mate

DAN. But if Smudge is the level we're dealing with

PIDGE. Na don't give it all that

SMUDGE. What's that?

DAN. I'm / just saying

PIDGE. Cos yer got a fuckin degree, well done

SMUDGE. What are you sayin?

PIDGE. University of Essex, fuck off

DAN. I'm just saying you're maybe not best placed to say, that's all

PIDGE. And you are, like?

SMUDGE. I ain't Einstein I know but I knew Frankie well as you

PIDGE. Better, probly.

DAN. (I doubt it)

PIDGE. You what?

DAN. I said I doubt it

PIDGE. How would you know?

PUGH. Don't start

PIDGE. These two went infants wiv him

PUGH. It's not a competition

PIDGE. I fuckin worked with him mate, day in day out

DAN. And he hated it!

PIDGE. Course he did; it's shit and we get paid peanuts, but that's what work is, ennit

DAN. Why?

PIDGE. Cos it's work. And that ain't the point is it

DAN. No

PIDGE. The point is I know Frankie better than you, / so don't

DAN. You knew.

PIDGE. You what?

DAN. You knew. Past tense.

PIDGE. Na I know him mate, I know him in here, I know him right the way down to the soles of my boots

DAN. That's what you think, is it?

PIDGE. That's what I know mate

DAN. Right

PIDGE. You got summink to say?

DAN. No, mate

PIDGE. Come on, Danny Big Bananas

DAN. You won't have scratched the surface, Pidge. It's morons like you that broke his heart.

PUGH. Alright

PIDGE. Say that again yer cunt

PUGH. Alright!

DAN. Because that's all you've got, isn't it? A haircut and a right hook.

PUGH. What is / the matter with

PIDGE. I'll fuckin show yer what I've got yer fuckin prick

PIDGE *goes to the edge of the wall and clumsily begins to lower himself off the side.*

PUGH. What are you doing?

PIDGE. I'm gonna shut him up once and for all

PUGH. Are you / seriously

DAN. Are you actually trying to start a fight?

PIDGE. I'm tryin to finish one

SMUDGE. Don't be stupid

DAN. You dick

SMUDGE. It's Frankie's / day

PUGH. Pidge

PIDGE. I don't care – how far am I off the floor?

PIDGE *is now at full extension hanging from the lip of the wall.*

PUGH. What?

PIDGE. How far am I off the floor?

PUGH. Look down and check

PIDGE. I've fuckin looked down ent I, I'm not a retard

PUGH. Then you know

PIDGE. Na I can't fuckin tell

PUGH. Why not?

PIDGE. I got one of me eyes covered, ent I

DAN. Oh that is / priceless

PUGH. Brilliant

PIDGE. Fuck off. Smudge, how far's the drop underneath me?

SMUDGE. Dunno. Couple of metres?

PIDGE. What's that in feet?

DAN. You're a roofer for a / living

PIDGE. You shut up. Is it safe to let go, Smudge?

SMUDGE. Dunno. You might hurt yourself

PIDGE. What's underneath me on this side?

SMUDGE. Just stones and that

PIDGE. What d'yer reckon?

SMUDGE. I wouldn't

PUGH. Just get back up

SMUDGE. Not in them shoes

PIDGE. Well I ain't got any others with me

PUGH. Come back up here, you tit

But PIDGE *is trying, the soles of his shoes keep slipping down the wall.*

DAN. Oh Christ

PUGH. Are you stuck?

PIDGE. No

PUGH. You are

PIDGE. I'm fuckin not, I'm just tryin not to scratch me suit up

DAN. You look ridiculous

PIDGE. You fuck right off, if I want your opinion I'll give it / to yer

PUGH. You do look ridiculous, Pidge

PIDGE. I'm in the wrong shoes, that's why

PUGH. Let go then

PIDGE. And break me ankle, yeah

DAN. Do you want a hand up?

PIDGE. No fuck off

PUGH. Give me your hand

PIDGE. Leave me alone.

Beat.

PIDGE *tries to assess the drop again. Decides against it. Hangs there.*

Beat.

This really hurts yer hands.

DAN. Here

PIDGE. Get off

DAN. I'm helping you

PIDGE. I don't need your help

SMUDGE. You do a bit

DAN. Come here

PIDGE. Get off me

> PIDGE *presses his foot into* DAN*'s hands, but does it quickly and messily so he can pretend he got back up by himself.*

See? Sorted.

DAN. Well that's told me

PIDGE. Right fuck this now, I'm goin for a shit

PUGH. Stay where you are

PIDGE. Na you ain't at work now – I've got a turtle's head, I bin waitin long enough, she can wait for me if she / turns up

PUGH. Don't be a prick

PIDGE. I ain't bein a prick, I either go now or shit in yer lap

PUGH. Be quick then

PIDGE. I ain't gonna have much of a choice am I

PUGH (*calling after him*). And bring us all a beer if you're going.

PIDGE. Get yer own yer lazy cunt!

PUGH. Oi!

PIDGE. You shoulda got me one earlier then, shouldn't yer?

PUGH. He's such a dick sometimes

SMUDGE. He'll bring em

PUGH. He won't. You know he won't.

> PUGH *pulls out his phone and checks the time.*

I'm gonna go get some.

SMUDGE. What about Kirsty?

PUGH. I'll be five minutes. Less. He's right, we need a toast for when we set the balloons off. You want another one?

SMUDGE. Yeah please.

PUGH. Dan?

DAN. No, I've barely touched this

PUGH. Alright.

Beat.

Listen, Dan, ignore Pidge. He's just.

DAN. I know.

PUGH. He's shitting himself.

DAN *smiles up at* PUGH.

Ha. I didn't even mean that.

DAN. I know what you mean.

Beat.

PUGH. Alright. Back in a minute

DAN. Pugh

PUGH. Yeah

DAN. Have you still got my lighter?

PUGH. Er, yeah…

He pats himself down and finds it.

Hang on.

He quickly finds his cigarettes and lights himself one.

SMUDGE. Pugh…

PUGH. No you can't have one.

SMUDGE. Alright.

PUGH. And don't tell Jenna.

He throws the lighter back to DAN.

DAN. Thanks. And congratulations mate. Again. That's really good news.

PUGH. Cheers. Yeah.

PUGH *goes.*

SMUDGE. D'you reckon?

DAN. Yeah.

SMUDGE. Me too. He'll be good married.

Beat.

Southend.

DAN. What?

SMUDGE (*calls off*). Pugh!

Beat.

Pugh!

Beat.

Pugh! He can't hear me. Southend ennit.

DAN. What is?

SMUDGE. Beginnin with 'S'.

DAN. Oh right. Yeah / maybe

SMUDGE. Shoulda got that ages ago

DAN. Yeah

SMUDGE. What a div.

Beat.

DAN. Can I tell you something, Smudge?

SMUDGE. Are you wearin fake tan?

DAN. What? No.

SMUDGE. Oh. What then?

Beat.

DAN. I was at the airport this morning. That's why I was late. I wasn't gonna come.

SMUDGE. Eh?

DAN. I got right up to the security gates.

SMUDGE. How come?

DAN....

Beat.

SMUDGE. Don't matter. You come in the end.

DAN. For my twelfth birthday my mum took us up to London.
Just me and Frankie. We wandered around, saw the sights, had
some lunch. Then went into Hamley's to get me a present.

SMUDGE. That the toy shop?

DAN. Yeah.

SMUDGE. Nice.

DAN. Yeah. It was. Yeah. But they had these people
demonstrating everything. The toys. Flying the planes and.
Driving the cars. And me and Frankie went up to this guy
doing magic. He must've been our age now, twenty-odd. Still
young. And he was doing this trick where he made money
disappear from a table. He just waved his hand over it and it
vanished. I thought it was brilliant. We stood there for about
five minutes watching him do it again and again and then
Frankie figured it out – he said: 'It's the ring. It's his ring, it's
magnetic.' But he sort of shouted it out. And this guy just
turned on him. Really tore him out. For ruining the trick.

SMUDGE *tuts.*

Yeah. Frankie wet himself. He scared him so much he
actually wet himself there and then.

Beat.

We were twelve. I mean that's way too old to... But neither
of us mentioned it. Ever. We never spoke about it. We just
pretended it didn't happen. Carried on walking around until
we found my mum and then went home. And that was it.

SMUDGE. You was always good at secrets. Both of yer.

Beat.

DAN. Yeah.

SMUDGE. He come round mine once nearly cryin. Some big
ruck wiv his dad.

DAN. About…?

SMUDGE *shrugs*.

SMUDGE. Wouldn't tell me. But it musta bin *big* big though.
He had all crusty blood in his nose.

DAN. His dad hit him?

SMUDGE. Right before his A levels come out, this was. 'S why
he never went uni.

DAN. What?

SMUDGE. Yeah. This row. Whatever it was. His old man said
he couldn't go after that.

DAN.…

SMUDGE. Probly money or summink I spose. He was gutted.
Proper gutted.

Beat.

Still. Sorted him out wiv his job, didn't he. And if he'd gone
uni he wouldna met Kirsty, so.

DAN. Yeah

SMUDGE. Y'know.

Beat.

The chime of the ice-cream van again.

D'you want one?

DAN. Hmm?

SMUDGE. Ice cream.

DAN. Oh. No.

SMUDGE. I might get one

DAN. Okay

SMUDGE. Get on the diet again tomorrow

DAN. Yeah

SMUDGE. I'm gonna get one. You sure you don't want one?

DAN. No. I'm fine

SMUDGE. Magnum?

DAN. No

SMUDGE. Mini Milk.

DAN. No

SMUDGE. Screwball?

DAN. Really

SMUDGE. Alright.

SMUDGE *stands.*

That's sort of a secret about Frankie and his dad.

DAN. Yeah. It's safe with me.

SMUDGE *nods and heads off to the ice-cream van, leaving*
DAN *alone.*

*He looks out at the water. Something rises in him. He closes
his eyes a moment.*

Then takes an envelope out of his pocket. Looks at it.

*He takes out a handwritten letter from inside and unfolds it.
He reads its contents, a lump in his throat.*

*Then he takes the lighter from his pocket and sets fire to the
bottom corner.*

As the flame begins to engulf the page, KIRSTY *arrives
above with a bunch of five black helium balloons. She stops
at the sight of* DAN, *who doesn't notice her.*

KIRSTY. What's that?

DAN *starts and looks at her, the letter burning between his
fingers.*

Beat.

Dan.

*The flame burns his hand and he flinches, dropping the letter
onto the sand, where it turns to ashes.*

DAN. You got them in the end / then

KIRSTY. Dan

Beat.

DAN. It was just. A work thing.

KIRSTY. It was handwritten.

DAN. Yeah. A memo. A note from.

KIRSTY....

DAN. I forgot I had it. It was in the suit, / so

KIRSTY. Why'd you burn it?

DAN. Why

KIRSTY. Why did you burn it?

DAN. What do you mean?

KIRSTY. I mean why did you fucking burn it?

Beat.

DAN. What are you

KIRSTY....

DAN. I just said. I found it, I burnt it, it's nothing

KIRSTY. A work thing

DAN. A yeah

KIRSTY. A memo

DAN. Yeah. A memo. A thing from the tea boy. Scrap paper.

KIRSTY....

DAN. I was bored, so.

Beat.

Kirsty.

Beat.

KIRSTY. Sorry. People are saying things / and

DAN. I know. I heard.

KIRSTY. I think it's. Getting to me.

DAN. You know that's all just.

KIRSTY....

DAN. He'd be here if he could.

KIRSTY. Yeah. Anything to kick around with you lot eh?

DAN *smiles*.

Where are they?

DAN. Oh just getting drinks and

KIRSTY....

DAN. They won't be long. Do you want one?

KIRSTY. No I've had... I don't even know. It's not helping

DAN. No

KIRSTY. I could drink the Thames and I'd still be

DAN....

KIRSTY. Not that that's alcoholic, but

DAN. I know what you mean

KIRSTY. Yeah? Makes one of us.

DAN *smiles*.

I'm all over the place, Dan.

DAN....

KIRSTY. I haven't cried all day. I can't. I've tried.

DAN. That might a good thing.

KIRSTY. No. I thought that but no, I don't think it is, I think one day I'll drown in it instead. All there is is anger. I'm fucking... angry, Dan. At him, at me, at everyone else. That's why I. I'm angry that it won't come out, the, the whatever, the, it won't go anywhere – I can't get it to go anywhere – which is just making me even more angry. Today of all days

I'm angry and it's shit because I keep looking around and seeing people talking and laughing and checking their phones and doing things that aren't even anything to do with Frankie and then someone says something and out of nowhere they all cry and someone else pats them on the back and says it's gonna be alright and it's not, it's not gonna be alright is it, ever, it's always gonna be like this from now on, with a gap, just a gaping hole everywhere you look and what about that is alright?

DAN....

KIRSTY. Nothing. And I can't even cry about it. And whenever someone else does I wanna claw their fucking eyes out and scream how they haven't got the right.

Beat.

I'm basically just being an arsehole

DAN. No you're / not

KIRSTY. And I really, really want to not be.

Beat.

The last time I saw him we had a row.

DAN....

KIRSTY. But then I phoned him later. Late. I'd been in bed for a bit and then I called. To make sure he was okay.

DAN. And

KIRSTY. And he was, he was fine, he picked up and we spoke for a bit and.

DAN....

KIRSTY. And I told him I loved him. Actually. For the first time in ages. Just because we didn't say it much, not for

DAN. Yeah

KIRSTY. And he said it back. And that he'd be home soon. And that was it.

Beat.

DAN. That's nice.

KIRSTY. Yeah. I'm pleased it finished up like that.

PIDGE and PUGH *return above –* PUGH *carrying beers,*
PIDGE waving his phone in front of PUGH's *face.*

PUGH. I don't want to see your shit, Pidge!

PIDGE. But it was like a chair leg, look, came out the water

PUGH. Jesus / Christ

PIDGE. Kirsty.

KIRSTY. Hello

PIDGE. We ready to do it then?

KIRSTY. Not really.

PIDGE. Oh

KIRSTY. But yeah. I think so.

Then SMUDGE, *returning with a 99 with Flake:*

SMUDGE. Southend!

PUGH. Eh?

SMUDGE. Beginnin wiv 'S'

PUGH. No

SMUDGE. Oh!

PIDGE. Fuck me, you still on that?

SMUDGE. Kirsty. Alright?

KIRSTY. Hello Smudge

PIDGE notices SMUDGE's *ice cream.*

PIDGE. Oh you have got to be fuckin / kiddin me

SMUDGE. You've took your make-up off

PIDGE. Pughie

He points to SMUDGE's *ice cream.*

KIRSTY. Er. / Yeah.

PUGH. Smudge…

SMUDGE. Na I liked it that's all

PUGH. Smudge

SMUDGE. Yeah?

PUGH *indicates his ice cream*.

Beat.

I didn't get the sprinkles.

PIDGE. Fuckin

PUGH. Unbelievable

SMUDGE. Sorry

PUGH. No don't be / sorry

PIDGE. Give it here

SMUDGE *holds it out*.

PUGH. No leave him. You have it Smudge

SMUDGE. I'll share it if yer want?

PUGH. No / just

PIDGE. No thanks

PUGH. Just stop there. Yeah?

SMUDGE. Alright

KIRSTY. Does anyone mind…?

Beat.

PUGH. Sorry. Yeah. Here.

PUGH *takes four of the five balloons and dishes them out to the other boys*.

Long beat.

PIDGE. Does someone wanna say summink?

PUGH. Not you

PIDGE. I didn't say me, did I

PUGH. Good. Kirsty?

KIRSTY. No I'm still not. Right. Dan?

DAN....

KIRSTY. Just you didn't speak earlier

PIDGE. Yeah you never did yer

PUGH. Oi

KIRSTY. You don't have to if

DAN. No, I'll.

Beat.

SMUDGE. (Shingle)

PUGH....

SMUDGE. (Shingle, Pugh)

PUGH. (Not now)

SMUDGE. (Is it though?)

PIDGE. Oh give it up will yer!

PUGH. You've said shingle.

SMUDGE. Have I?

PUGH. Yeah. Dan.

PIDGE. Just put him out of his misery

PUGH. Not now

KIRSTY. Are you lot playing I Spy?

SMUDGE. Yeah

PIDGE. They are, not me

PUGH. Sorry, it's. It's just gone on a while.

KIRSTY. What is it?

PUGH....

KIRSTY. Beginning with 'S' did you say?

PUGH. Yeah

KIRSTY. Steps.

PUGH. Er. No

KIRSTY. Stairs.

PUGH. No

KIRSTY. Sky.

> PUGH *shakes his head*.

> Skies.

> PUGH *shakes his head*.

> Shore. Shoreline. Stones. Sticks. Shingle. Shingles. Skin. Scars. Scabs. Stubble. Shaving rash. Sideburns. Shirts. Shirtsleeves. Stomachs. Shiny suits

PUGH. No

KIRSTY. Silly little boys. A shower of shit.

> *Beat*.

> Someone missing.

PUGH. No

KIRSTY. Something else then?

PUGH.…

KIRSTY. Something else, Pugh?

PUGH. Yeah

KIRSTY. What then? I give up.

PUGH. Look, Kirst

KIRSTY. What is it?

PUGH.…

KIRSTY. Pugh

PIDGE. Come on

KIRSTY. Tell me

PUGH. It doesn't matter

KIRSTY. Tell me. You spy with your little eye…

Long beat.

Pugh

PUGH. Sod-all.

They all just stand there a moment.

Then KIRSTY *smiles. She finally looks like she might cry.*

End of Part One.

PART TWO

One

KIRSTY *holding a shop-bought birthday cake with one lit candle. FRANKIE – bleary eyed but fully clothed – has just been woken up.*

They look at each other, until:

KIRSTY. Come on then, do something.

FRANKIE. What time is it?

KIRSTY. Half six? Just gone?

FRANKIE....

KIRSTY. Yeah I know, but.

He retches. Just about holds it down.

Whoa, fucking hell, you alright?

FRANKIE *nods.*

You sure? Do you want me to get you a bowl?

FRANKIE *shakes his head. Then nods, beckoning for a bowl. As she goes:*

Don't get it on the bed, I've just changed it.

FRANKIE *poised, not sure which way it's gonna go...*

Until KIRSTY *returns with a washing-up bowl and hands it over. The wave passes.* FRANKIE *lays back and catches his breath a moment.*

Alright?

FRANKIE. I think so, yeah.

KIRSTY. Sure?

FRANKIE *nods*.

Big night then?

FRANKIE. Yeah. Sort of.

KIRSTY. Must've been; I haven't seen you like this since…

FRANKIE.…

KIRSTY. I can't remember

FRANKIE. No

KIRSTY. It's good; you need a blowout once in a while. What happened to staying at Dan's?

FRANKIE. Mmn?

KIRSTY. I thought you were staying at Dan's.

FRANKIE. Yeah no.

KIRSTY.…

FRANKIE. He's moving, so.

KIRSTY. Is he?

FRANKIE. Yeah.

KIRSTY. Dan is? Where to?

FRANKIE. Hong Kong.

KIRSTY. Wow.

FRANKIE. Yeah.

KIRSTY. Fucking hell, I thought you were gonna say Rayleigh or something.

FRANKIE. I know.

KIRSTY. What for? For work?

FRANKIE *nods*.

For how long?

FRANKIE. For. Ever. I think.

KIRSTY. What, soon?

FRANKIE. Two weeks.

KIRSTY. So… why didn't you stay at his?

FRANKIE. He's. Just. He's packing.

KIRSTY. Already?

FRANKIE. Said his stuff's

KIRSTY. Keen-o.

FRANKIE. Yeah.

KIRSTY. Well good luck to him. I wouldn't fancy it.

FRANKIE. No?

KIRSTY. No thanks. Would you?

FRANKIE.…

KIRSTY. Frankie, you get nervous if you leave Southend.

FRANKIE. No I don't.

KIRSTY. You get lost in Lakeside, can you imagine what you'd
    be like in Hong Kong?

FRANKIE.…

KIRSTY. At least you'd be a bit taller. Compared.

FRANKIE. Thanks

KIRSTY. Come on

    *She presents him with the cake again (relighting the candle if
    it's gone out).*

FRANKIE. What's the time?

KIRSTY. Twenty-five to seven? I know; but I didn't think you'd
    be here, and you are, so.

FRANKIE.…

KIRSTY. I wanted to see you blow your candles out. Well.
    Candle.

FRANKIE. Right.

> FRANKIE *goes to blow the candle out.*

KIRSTY. Hang on, you've got to make a wish!

FRANKIE....

KIRSTY. Frankie. Play the game.

FRANKIE. Sorry, yeah.

> *He closes his eyes, wishing.*

> *Long beat. Bit too long.*

KIRSTY. Have you fallen asleep?

FRANKIE. Sorry, no

> *He opens his eyes.*

KIRSTY. Go on then.

> *He blows the candle out.*

> *Beat.*

What d'you wish for?

FRANKIE. No I can't

KIRSTY. Tell me

FRANKIE. I can't

KIRSTY. Boring.

> *Beat*

FRANKIE. Are you wearing lipstick?

KIRSTY. Yeah?

FRANKIE....

KIRSTY. Nearly forgot, don't move.

> *She exits.* FRANKIE *looks after her a moment, confused somehow.*

> *Then he checks his phone. Nothing.*

KIRSTY *returns, hands behind her back.*

KIRSTY. Close your eyes again.

FRANKIE. What for?

KIRSTY. Close them.

He does.

She produces a small gift-wrapped box and puts it in his hands.

He opens his eyes and looks at it.

FRANKIE. What's this?

KIRSTY. Open it you div.

A car horn beep-beeps outside.

Ah shitbags

FRANKIE. What

KIRSTY. Quick

FRANKIE. What

KIRSTY. I'm late

FRANKIE. Late?

KIRSTY. Yeah, quick

FRANKIE. How can. / It's half past

KIRSTY. Have you seen my – what? Have you seen my keys?

FRANKIE. It's half past six

KIRSTY. Well it's twenty to seven

FRANKIE. Alright. You don't start work / till

KIRSTY. Keys, Frank, can you help me look?

FRANKIE. I don't understand.

KIRSTY. My keys

FRANKIE. No I mean

KIRSTY. I'm getting a lift in, so

FRANKIE. A lift?

KIRSTY. Yeah

FRANKIE. Who from?

KIRSTY. Greg. Can you help me please?

FRANKIE. Greg?

KIRSTY. Greg. Greg Edwards.

FRANKIE.…

KIRSTY. They recommend it, don't they? Environment people. And it means you can have the car

FRANKIE. What for?

KIRSTY. For your other present.

FRANKIE.…

KIRSTY. I've booked you the day off.

Beat.

FRANKIE. Why?

KIRSTY. Because. It's your birthday

FRANKIE. But. I mean.

KIRSTY. Alright then, go to work

FRANKIE. No, / no

KIRSTY. I thought you'd rather do something nice. I've booked us lunch. A new place near the school. Giuseppi's. Glovanni's

FRANKIE. Right

KIRSTY. For four.

FRANKIE. Four?

KIRSTY. O'clock. Not people.

FRANKIE. That's. Dinner. Almost

KIRSTY. Late lunch then

FRANKIE. I could've gone to work

KIRSTY. Then go to work, do what you want Frankie.

The car horn again.

Look, I've got to go – can I take your keys?

As he fishes them out of his pocket:

The car keys are on mine when you find them. You still haven't opened your present.

FRANKIE. No, the tape's

KIRSTY. Quickly

FRANKIE. I can open it later

KIRSTY. Nono open it now, you might need it later.

FRANKIE. Why?

KIRSTY. Because you might.

FRANKIE. Why might I?

KIRSTY. You just might!

FRANKIE. Why though?

KIRSTY. So you can be on time for a change!

FRANKIE. It's. What, is it a watch?

KIRSTY. Why d'you always have to spoil it?

The car horn beeps again.

FRANKIE. Does he know what time it is?

KIRSTY. Well he better do, yeah; he's got the same one.

FRANKIE....

KIRSTY. Joke.

FRANKIE. Sorry, I'm.

KIRSTY. Don't worry about it.

She kisses him and starts to leave.

Have a nice day, yeah? And don't forget to find the keys before you go out anywhere. And if you get a minute I think there's something gone off at the back of the fridge, but only if you get a minute.

FRANKIE.…

KIRSTY. What's wrong?

FRANKIE. No nothing. Tired. Hungover. Pissed.

KIRSTY. Alright.

FRANKIE. You?

KIRSTY. Me?

FRANKIE. Yeah are you alright?

KIRSTY. Yeah?

FRANKIE. Yeah?

KIRSTY. Yeah.

FRANKIE. Good.

KIRSTY. I mean I'm not the one

FRANKIE.…

KIRSTY. Make sure you drink plenty of water and I'll see you in a bit, alright?

Beat.

FRANKIE. Alright.

KIRSTY. Are you.

FRANKIE.…

KIRSTY. Are you sure you're alright?

Two

PIDGE *and* FRANKIE *in a greasy spoon.*

PIDGE. Cos you look like shit mate.

FRANKIE. Thanks.

PIDGE. You do though. Like an actual shit. Like a turd in a shirt.

FRANKIE....

PIDGE. You shoulda done what I done and had a tactical vom last night. Schoolboy.

FRANKIE. Yeah I know.

PIDGE. 'S alright, get a bit of grub in yer, yer'll perk up

FRANKIE. I don't think I can

PIDGE. Don't be stupid, I've already ordered you a bacon sarnie en I

FRANKIE. Thanks, but

PIDGE. Come off it, it's yer birthday present

FRANKIE. I can't

PIDGE. Don't be so fuckin ungrateful

FRANKIE. I'm not being ungrateful

PIDGE. Then eat it then

FRANKIE. I can't Pidge

PIDGE. Eat it

FRANKIE. No

PIDGE. Fuckin eat it

FRANKIE. Pidge

PIDGE. Alright fuck yer then, I'll take it wiv me for lunch. You sittin down today or what?

FRANKIE. I might just.

He gestures off.

PIDGE. I wouldn't go in there mate. Specially not to be sick. You don't wanna put yer face near what I've just done.

FRANKIE. Fuck's sake.

PIDGE. I had the chilli sauce again last night

FRANKIE. You went to Charcoal Grill?

PIDGE. Yeah I was wiv that bird weren't I, the little blonde one wi the forehead, and she was havin it – that and the garlic sauce an all. I mean there's etiquette ent there?

FRANKIE. Yeah?

PIDGE. Here, guess who else was in there?

FRANKIE. Who?

PIDGE. Smudge.

FRANKIE. Smudge?

PIDGE. Sittin there in the corner when I walked in: fuckin quarter pounder wi cheesy chips in front of him – had his arm round it like I was about to copy his homework or summink.

FRANKIE. He told me he was going home.

PIDGE. Yeah well it might as well be his fuckin ome, mightn't it, the amount e's in there

FRANKIE. Someone needs to talk to him

PIDGE. Oh fuck im, he's alright en e? Fat people are jolly.

FRANKIE. He won't be when he has a heart attack at forty.

PIDGE. Na well that's his fault though, ennit; he dies young, he dies young. There's only about four people who'd notice anyway. Come on, sit the fuck down will yer, yer makin me nervous.

FRANKIE *does, tentatively.*

So happy day off then, yer cunt. What yer doin all day?

FRANKIE. I don't know.

PIDGE. Lucky fucker, yer shoulda stayed in bed.

FRANKIE. Yeah. Kirsty woke me up.

PIDGE. Course she did; birthday blowie. Get anyfin else?

FRANKIE. Erm. Yeah. Well.

He takes his new watch from his pocket. It's massive. Or brightly coloured. Or both.

PIDGE. Fuck me, look at that – you goin scuba-divin or summink?

FRANKIE. No.

PIDGE. Na only jokin, I like it. It's big. From the wife is it?

FRANKIE. Yeah.

PIDGE. Put it on.

FRANKIE. Don't. Call her that please

PIDGE. Why not?

FRANKIE. Just.

PIDGE. Only a matter of time mate

FRANKIE. You think so?

PIDGE. Yeah. How the fuck do I know? But yeah. Obviously.

FRANKIE. Yeah.

Beat.

PIDGE. Here, have I told you my joke?

FRANKIE. Which one?

PIDGE. Bloke goes into a chippy with a / cod under his arm

   PIDGE *does a little teapot arm to indicate the fish.*

FRANKIE. You've told me it, yeah

PIDGE. He says:

FRANKIE. I know

PIDGE. 'Sorry mate, do you sell fishcakes?' Says 'Yeah.' He says 'Nice one…

He points to the imaginary fish under his arm.

…cos it's / his birthday.'

FRANKIE. / It's his birthday. That's your fish joke, I must've heard it a hundred times

PIDGE. Well yeah alright, but it's relevant ennit?

FRANKIE. How is it?

PIDGE. It's yer birthday.

FRANKIE. I'm not a cod

PIDGE. Well na, but. Yer smell like one. Speakin of which: that bird.

FRANKIE. I don't want to know.

PIDGE. Na yer don't.

He shakes his head at the thought.

Top night though anyway.

FRANKIE. Yeah.

PIDGE. Fuckin Dan, springin that. Are you gonna, like, miss him and that? Cos I reckon I might be a bit fuckin… thingy. When he goes. Not thingy but y'know. Not in a gay way, but it's us, ennit, it's always bin, like, us. Us lot. Won't be the same wi someone else. Good player an all, the prick. Part from his penalties. Don't go and tell him I said that, like.

FRANKIE. Yeah, no. My lips arc scaled.

FRANKIE *checks his phone.*

PIDGE. What am I keepin you from yer busy day of fuck-all?

FRANKIE. No, just. Shouldn't you be on site by now?

PIDGE. Were you just checkin the time?

FRANKIE. Why?

PIDGE. Why? You got fuckin Big Ben strapped to yer wrist!

FRANKIE. I think it'll just take a little while to get used to

PIDGE. I'll go in a minute. The Liff's alright for half hour

FRANKIE. The what?

PIDGE. Igor, whatever his name is – the new boy

FRANKIE. Ivan

PIDGE. Lithuanian en e.

FRANKIE. He's Latvian.

PIDGE. Is he? Same thing

FRANKIE. Not really.

PIDGE. He can't speak a word anyway can he, I'll call him
    what I like – he won't know the difference

FRANKIE. Have you actually spoken to him yet?

PIDGE. Na

FRANKIE. He's nice

PIDGE. Alright yer queer

FRANKIE. I'm just saying

PIDGE. He's still a Liff.

FRANKIE. He's not

PIDGE. Whatever he is.

FRANKIE. If I was.

    Beat.

    I mean, if

PIDGE. Spit it out

FRANKIE. If that was me.

PIDGE. If what was you?

FRANKIE. If I was Latvian do you think we'd still be mates?

PIDGE. You what?

FRANKIE. Or Lithuanian

PIDGE. But yer not though are yer

FRANKIE. But if I was

PIDGE. Yeah but yer not though

FRANKIE. No. If I was. Still me, just Latvian.

PIDGE. But then you wouldn't be you would yer

FRANKIE. I just mean

PIDGE. Na you're you cos I know yer, like – we've got stuff in common. In our bones and that, since kids. He comes to work wiv his boiled potatoes and his cabbage for lunch and listenin to fuckin techno on his portable-radio thing, I ain't got a clue where that comes from have I? I don't mean literally like, Lithuania or whatever

FRANKIE. Latvia

PIDGE. Whatever, I'm just sayin I ain't never gonna *know* him am I, is what I'm sayin – not proply like. It's tribal, ennit. Yer either us or you ain't, and fair do's if you ain't, just don't expect to be treated like you are, that's all, know what I mean?

FRANKIE. ...

PIDGE. Course yer do cos yer one of us, intcher.

FRANKIE. ...

PIDGE. Intcher.

FRANKIE. Yeah.

PIDGE. An if you ain't – if yer the Liff or whatever – yer must look around this place an think to yerself: 'You mug. What are you doin here?'

Three

FRANKIE *and* KIRSTY *in a primary-school classroom.*

KIRSTY. Frankie?

FRANKIE. Mmn?

KIRSTY. I said what are you doing here?

FRANKIE. Sorry, yeah. I found your keys

KIRSTY. My keys?

FRANKIE. They were in the kitchen.

Beat.

KIRSTY. Okay. Have you come here just to / tell me

FRANKIE. Guess where

KIRSTY. What?

FRANKIE. Guess where your keys were

KIRSTY. In the kitchen

FRANKIE. Yeah but where?

KIRSTY. I don't know

FRANKIE. Guess then

KIRSTY. On the side, I don't know – you can't be here Frankie.

Beat.

FRANKIE. Why not?

KIRSTY. Because.

FRANKIE. Because

KIRSTY. There are rules.

FRANKIE. What rules?

KIRSTY. You have to sign in and get a badge / and

FRANKIE. Yeah but

KIRSTY. Have you signed in?

FRANKIE. No

KIRSTY. Have you got a badge?

FRANKIE. No. Well… my nan sent me a card with one on, / but.

KIRSTY. Frankie.

FRANKIE. No it's fine I'm not staying

KIRSTY. It doesn't matter how long you're here for, / there's a protocol

FRANKIE. There's hundreds of them, eh?

Beat.

KIRSTY. Hundreds of…

FRANKIE. Kids.

KIRSTY. Well / yeah

FRANKIE. It is like a little tribe, he's right

KIRSTY. Who's – what are you talking about?

FRANKIE. All chatting away like they've decided what they think

KIRSTY. Did you just come in through the playground?

FRANKIE. Yeah. It's like they know who they are / already

KIRSTY. You can't just walk through a playground, Frankie!

FRANKIE. No, it's fine

KIRSTY. I don't think their parents would think / it's

FRANKIE. It's fine, I saw Greg. He waved.

KIRSTY. He what?

FRANKIE. He waved.

KIRSTY. Who did? / Greg?

FRANKIE. Greg, yeah he waved.

KIRSTY. Did he?

FRANKIE. Yeah he was on duty and he waved.

KIRSTY. Right.

FRANKIE. What.

KIRSTY. No nothing.

FRANKIE. So it's fine.

KIRSTY. No it's, no, stop saying it's fine!

FRANKIE. It is though!

KIRSTY. Frankie!

FRANKIE. Sorry. I just. I didn't think it'd be a problem

KIRSTY. Well it is. So.

　　Beat.

FRANKIE. I've never come here, have I? Inside.

KIRSTY. Because you're not a teacher. Or a child under ten.

FRANKIE. No, but I'm your.

KIRSTY. So? I've never come to your work. What's the difference?

FRANKIE. You don't like heights. And we move / about

KIRSTY. I don't not come to your work because I don't like heights – I don't come to your work because it's work.

FRANKIE. Does Greg bring his missus in?

KIRSTY.…

FRANKIE. For example.

KIRSTY. No! What are you – this isn't a restaurant, Frankie. Or a cinema, or

FRANKIE. Or our front room.

KIRSTY. Yeah. No. What?

FRANKIE. Cos I mean we don't do anything, do we?

KIRSTY. Such as?

FRANKIE. I mean. Anything.

KIRSTY. Like

FRANKIE. Go out. Do things.

KIRSTY. We're going to a restaurant today!

FRANKIE. Cos it's my birthday, yeah

KIRSTY. Well then let's not bother then

FRANKIE. I'm not saying that, / I'm

KIRSTY. What are you saying, Frankie? Have you just come down here to pick a fight or something?

FRANKIE. No! The opposite

KIRSTY. Then what do you want? You're gonna get me in trouble

FRANKIE. I dunno I was just thinking.

KIRSTY. What

FRANKIE. What do you think about going away?

KIRSTY.…

FRANKIE. Spain, maybe. Or Turkey

KIRSTY. You are joking?

FRANKIE. No?

KIRSTY. That's.

Beat.

FRANKIE. What

KIRSTY. That is. For months I – forget it

FRANKIE. No, what

KIRSTY. I was saying for months I was trying to get you to book, from Jesus I don't know about January through to May I was saying let's book a holiday, and as soon as I'm back at work / you're all

FRANKIE. I didn't mean. I don't mean a holiday. I mean. Y'know. For a bit. To

KIRSTY. To

FRANKIE. To. Yeah, to live. For a bit. Give it a go.

Beat.

KIRSTY. Have you lost your (fucking) mind?

FRANKIE....

KIRSTY. Where has this come from?

FRANKIE. I dunno, / I just

KIRSTY. Obviously

FRANKIE. Just something Pidge said

KIRSTY. Pidge?

FRANKIE. Yeah

KIRSTY. Pidge thinks we should move abroad?

FRANKIE. No, / he

KIRSTY. With all the foreigners?

FRANKIE. No he never said that

KIRSTY. What did he say? Actually I don't care what he said; I'm not moving abroad, Frankie.

FRANKIE. Alright

KIRSTY. Just like that?

FRANKIE. No, we. We could. Plan it, / or

KIRSTY. I don't want to, apart from anything else.

Beat.

FRANKIE. No. Fair enough. Just a thought.

Beat.

KIRSTY. Look I wasn't gonna say anything yet – not until it's definite – and I can't even talk about it now – but this fast-track thing. The thing I told you about, to be a senior teacher – I said I wasn't sure / but

FRANKIE. Yeah no I know the thing

KIRSTY. It looks like I'm gonna get it. Greg applied without me knowing and now the school are gonna pay, so.

FRANKIE.…

KIRSTY. I couldn't even if I wanted / to

FRANKIE. Right

KIRSTY. It's good news

FRANKIE. Yeah. No yeah

KIRSTY. More money / and

FRANKIE. Yeah no, that's. Yeah. It's really good news. Congratulations

KIRSTY. Well. It's not definite / yet

FRANKIE. No, but.

KIRSTY. I'll talk to you about it later at lunch, yeah?

FRANKIE. Dinner.

KIRSTY. Yeah late lunch, whatever.

A bell rings to signal the end of break.

Frankie

FRANKIE. Yeah I'll go. They were in the fridge by the way. Your keys. You must've. I dunno. But I couldn't smell anything off, / so

KIRSTY. I'll get them off you later, okay?

FRANKIE. I like your lipstick. I didn't say it this morning. It's nice.

KIRSTY. Okay.

FRANKIE.…

KIRSTY. Frankie. Are you ever getting out of here?

Four

FRANKIE *and* SMUDGE *in* SMUDGE*'s bedroom.*

SMUDGE. Doubt it mate

FRANKIE. No I mean it, Smudge

Beat.

SMUDGE. Who wiv?

FRANKIE. Some bloke from her work

SMUDGE. Who?

FRANKIE. Greg something / he's called

SMUDGE. You sure?

FRANKIE. I think so

SMUDGE. Like double sure?

FRANKIE. No. Not. / No, but

SMUDGE. Well then

FRANKIE. There's just something about her.

SMUDGE. What?

FRANKIE. I dunno. It's like

SMUDGE....

FRANKIE. It's like a light's come on or something

SMUDGE. What's that mean?

Beat.

FRANKIE. My mum met someone once

SMUDGE. Yer mum did?

FRANKIE. Yeah. We must've been… Year 10? Someone she worked with. I saw them outside her office

SMUDGE. Shit

FRANKIE. No. A bit of me was praying she'd. Go for it. Actually. Say fuck it, and

SMUDGE. Yeah?

FRANKIE. Yeah a bit of me, yeah

SMUDGE. So what happened?

FRANKIE. Nothing.

Beat.

SMUDGE. What d'yer mean?

FRANKIE. Just. Nothing happened, after that. She saw me standing there and so I went over and I met him. And he was nice. And that was it. It just went away.

SMUDGE. How d'yer know?

FRANKIE. She just smiled a bit less and went to work a bit later and. Stopped wearing make-up again.

SMUDGE. …

FRANKIE. Like before. I think she thought she'd made her bed, so

SMUDGE. Yer dad ever find out?

FRANKIE *shakes his head.*

FRANKIE. I mean that might have been it. The start of something. A whole new fucking…

SMUDGE. She's alright though ain't she?

FRANKIE. …

SMUDGE. Yer mum

FRANKIE. She's. Yeah, she's.

Beat.

Yeah. She's 'alright'.

Long beat.

SMUDGE. D'you wanna play Fifa?

FRANKIE. Not for the minute.

Long beat.

SMUDGE. Little while ago, right, I went up in the loft. It was
ages ago actually. Anyway. I found this box of old letters
what my dad had writ to my mum. From. Kuwait I think. Is
that what it's called?

FRANKIE. Kuwait?

SMUDGE. Yeah.

FRANKIE. Yeah.

SMUDGE. Kuwait?

FRANKIE. Yeah.

SMUDGE. Sounds weird.

FRANKIE. It's right.

SMUDGE. Kuwait?

FRANKIE. Yeah.

SMUDGE. Kuwait.

FRANKIE. Kuwait.

SMUDGE. Kuwait. Yeah. He was stationed there or summink.
So I found this box with letters in his writing. From there.
You could smell em and that. Proper old. So I got em down
and showed me mum. She'd read em, like, when he sent em,
but. She went anyway – cried and that. I felt a bit bad. But
one letter had a poem in it. You know what I'm like: I hate
poems and foreign films and that. But I read it anyway. And
it was like…

SMUDGE *shrugs*.

Dunno. Massive. Not long. It weren't that long. But it was
massive. Bout him and my mum. I didn't know people
thought like that. Not in real life. Yer never hear it, do yer?
But he was like. Full of it. All there in the words, writ down,
like that.

FRANKIE. Nice

SMUDGE. Yeah. Dunno where that went. I ain't even never
even writ a letter, have you?

FRANKIE. Er. Yeah. Well. Like one, ever

SMUDGE. This was proper. And them two met when they was
eleven. So.

Beat.

FRANKIE. So…

SMUDGE. Some people get it right early doors, that's all. They
know.

FRANKIE. Yeah.

SMUDGE. Like you and Kirsty.

FRANKIE *nods.*

You're welcome.

FRANKIE *smiles.*

That a new watch?

FRANKIE. Oh. Yeah

SMUDGE. Has it got a calculator?

FRANKIE. No.

SMUDGE. Oh.

Beat.

Oh shit.

FRANKIE. What?

SMUDGE. Hang on.

SMUDGE *rummages somewhere…*

FRANKIE. What are you doing?

SMUDGE. Here y'are. Happy birthday. Sorry.

He holds out a Kinder Egg.

It's a Kinder Egg.

FRANKIE. Where'd you get that?

SMUDGE. Open it.

FRANKIE. Are these on your diet?

SMUDGE. I only buy em for the toy.

FRANKIE. And what about your burger?

SMUDGE....

FRANKIE. Pidge told me he saw you last night.

Beat.

SMUDGE. You see that girl he was wiv? Was she a midget d'you fink?

FRANKIE. No

SMUDGE. She had the big forehead and / that

FRANKIE. Smudge

SMUDGE. Never see em any more do yer? Midgets. D'you reckon they're goin extinct?

FRANKIE. Stop changing the subject. You won't make old bones if you carry on

SMUDGE. 'S alright. 'Live hard, die young', all that.

FRANKIE. And what about the rest of us?

SMUDGE. What.

FRANKIE. What would we do without you?

SMUDGE *shrugs.*

SMUDGE. Same thing as now, probably. Dan's off en e? China

FRANKIE. Hong Kong

SMUDGE. Yeah, so. Just one less ennit.

Beat.

Does he like sushi?

FRANKIE. Dan? I think so, yeah.

SMUDGE. Lucky. I don't. I hate it. Never had it.

FRANKIE. How do you know then?

SMUDGE *shrugs*.

SMUDGE. What d'ya get?

FRANKIE. Erm. A –

FRANKIE *shows him whatever it is in the egg*.

SMUDGE. Oh.

FRANKIE. Yeah.

SMUDGE. Bit…

FRANKIE. Aren't they always?

SMUDGE. Na I got a monkey once. You could wind it up.

FRANKIE *smiles*.

What.

FRANKIE. No. Just. Are you. I dunno.

SMUDGE.…

FRANKIE. D'you look around and think: 'Yeah.'

SMUDGE *shrugs*.

SMUDGE. Yeah? Why not?

FRANKIE. Why not.

Beat.

SMUDGE. You gonna ask her d'you fink?

FRANKIE. Ask…

SMUDGE. Kirsty. About

FRANKIE. No. No. I dunno. Do you think I should?

SMUDGE. Na.

FRANKIE. No?

SMUDGE. Na it's nuffin I reckon. Probly just likes his car or summink.

Beat.

FRANKIE. Do you think she'd ever. Leave me, / or

SMUDGE. Na.

FRANKIE. No, nor do I.

SMUDGE. Just like you wouldn't leave her.

Beat.

FRANKIE. Do me a favour, Smudge? Don't tell the boys.

SMUDGE. Course not. Nuffin to tell.

FRANKIE. Yeah. No. Right.

SMUDGE. So.

Beat.

Unless you did ask her.

FRANKIE. What, you think I should then?

SMUDGE. Na. I'm just saying, you could.

FRANKIE. You think so?

SMUDGE. Dunno.

FRANKIE.…

SMUDGE. But what's the worst that could happen?

Five

FRANKIE *in a restaurant with a bottle of champagne.* KIRSTY *has just arrived.*

KIRSTY. I could kill myself

FRANKIE. No it's fine

KIRSTY. I'm really sorry

FRANKIE. It's really fine

KIRSTY. What time is it?

FRANKIE. You're not that late

KIRSTY. Ah, you're wearing your watch!

FRANKIE. Yeah

KIRSTY. You like it, then?

   Beat.

FRANKIE. Yeah

KIRSTY. You don't like it.

FRANKIE. Yeah. No, yeah, / it's

KIRSTY. You sure?

FRANKIE. Was it expensive?

   Beat.

KIRSTY. Was it expensive?

FRANKIE. No, it just. It looks expensive, you shouldn't / have

KIRSTY. It's not from the joint account or anything

FRANKIE. No I'm not. That's not what I'm saying

KIRSTY. Okay

FRANKIE. It just looks

KIRSTY. I wanted to get you something nice. So.

FRANKIE. Yeah. No. Thank you. It's lovely.

KIRSTY. Okay.

Beat.

Good. Okay.

FRANKIE. Yeah, cheers.

KIRSTY. Are you drinking wine?

FRANKIE. Er, yeah. Champagne actually. / I thought

KIRSTY. You don't like champagne.

FRANKIE. No I know / but

KIRSTY. Why are you drinking it then?

FRANKIE. You like it.

KIRSTY. But it's your birthday.

FRANKIE. Yeah, but.

KIRSTY....

FRANKIE. We're celebrating aren't we. Your senior-teacher thing

KIRSTY. Oh right

FRANKIE. Have a / glass

KIRSTY. Thanks

FRANKIE. It's nice

KIRSTY. But it's not confirmed / yet, so

FRANKIE. Sort of. For champagne

KIRSTY. I'm okay.

Beat.

FRANKIE. What?

KIRSTY. I'm fine actually. I'll just have a water or something.

Beat.

FRANKIE. Really?

KIRSTY. Yeah.

FRANKIE. How come?

KIRSTY. I just don't really want a drink, that's all. I don't feel like it.

FRANKIE. But I mean.

KIRSTY.…

FRANKIE. What?!

KIRSTY. I've got work to do

FRANKIE. Tonight?

KIRSTY. Yeah I'm behind on lesson plans, so

FRANKIE.…

KIRSTY. You're at football anyway aren't you?

FRANKIE. Yeah, / but.

KIRSTY. So.

Beat.

It's a Monday night – afternoon, even. And it's not like it's a big birthday.

Beat.

Sorry, I didn't know you were gonna buy it

FRANKIE. No it's

KIRSTY. We can have a nice time without me drinking

FRANKIE. Yeah, I know

KIRSTY. So

FRANKIE. Yeah

Beat.

KIRSTY. Are you hungry then? I'm starving.

FRANKIE. Where did you say you've been?

KIRSTY.…

FRANKIE. If you've not been working?

KIRSTY. I have

FRANKIE. But you said you're behind

KIRSTY. No I've been at work, I've just not been doing lesson plans

FRANKIE. So.

KIRSTY. ...

FRANKIE. What were you doing?

Beat.

KIRSTY. Look I've said I'm sorry I was late

FRANKIE. It's fine

KIRSTY. Well it's obviously not

FRANKIE. No it is, it's / fine

KIRSTY. There's an application thing, a sort of package to put together, for / this

FRANKIE. Right

KIRSTY. So I was getting some help with that.

FRANKIE. From...

Beat.

KIRSTY. Just a couple of. Why are you looking at / me like

FRANKIE. Can I ask you something?

KIRSTY. Yeah?

FRANKIE. ...

KIRSTY. Sounds.

FRANKIE. ...

KIRSTY. What.

FRANKIE. Do you wanna get married?

KIRSTY. ...

FRANKIE. I'm not. This isn't, like. I mean is that something you want?

KIRSTY. Okay

FRANKIE. You don't have to answer now. I just / mean

KIRSTY. Yeah.

FRANKIE....

KIRSTY. You know I. Yeah. We've spoken about.

FRANKIE. Yeah. Well. Not lately

KIRSTY. No, but.

FRANKIE....

KIRSTY. Money's been a thing, but. Why? Are you saying you don't want / to

FRANKIE. No! No no, I was just. Checking

KIRSTY. Okay.

>   *Beat.*

>   Okay.

>   *Beat.*

>   I mean money's still a factor for now, but. When I get this thing. Or if I get this thing

FRANKIE. Yeah

KIRSTY. We could…

FRANKIE....

KIRSTY. Think about it anyway

FRANKIE. Yeah, no

KIRSTY. Easier than moving abroad!

>   *Beat.*

FRANKIE. Yeah. Sorry about before.

KIRSTY. No, I was just a bit caught off guard that's all. And there are all these rules if you / wanna

>   FRANKIE *laughs.*

>   What.

FRANKIE. No just. Rules.

KIRSTY. Yeah?

FRANKIE. Lots of rules. Endless rules because of where you are or.

Beat.

KIRSTY. What's going on Frankie?

FRANKIE.…

KIRSTY. You seem

FRANKIE. No. Nothing, sorry. Just.

KIRSTY.…

FRANKIE. I think I need some food.

KIRSTY. Yeah. Good. So. Food. Do you know what you want then?

FRANKIE.…

KIRSTY. Frankie. Do you know what you want?

Six

FRANKIE *and* PUGH *in a changing room.*

PUGH. Yes or no?

FRANKIE. Yeah. No.

PUGH. Why not?

FRANKIE. I haven't got kit

PUGH. I'll lend you kit

FRANKIE. And I'm. No, I've come from dinner. Lunch.
    Whatever.

PUGH. So?

FRANKIE. I'm just a bit

    Beat.

PUGH. Are you pissed?

FRANKIE. No, / but.

PUGH. You drove here, didn't you?

FRANKIE. Yeah, no, I'm not pissed

PUGH. What have you had?

FRANKIE. I just I bought a bottle of champagne and I haven't
    really / eaten

PUGH. How much have you had?

FRANKIE. Then Kirsty says she's not drinking, I mean. It's my
    birthday

PUGH. Did you drink the whole bottle?

FRANKIE. It's my fucking birthday and she wouldn't

PUGH. Frankie.

FRANKIE. I couldn't just. It cost a fortune.

PUGH. You're a dick.

FRANKIE. Yeah I know

PUGH. Gimme your keys.

FRANKIE. No I can't

PUGH. Give em

FRANKIE. They're not mine, I / need to

PUGH. Whose are they?

FRANKIE. Kirsty's. I forgot to give / them

PUGH. You're not driving back

FRANKIE. I'm fine

PUGH. I'll drop you

FRANKIE. I don't want

PUGH. I'll drop you

FRANKIE. Pugh, I need to…

Beat.

PUGH. What.

FRANKIE. Where are the others?

PUGH. This is it

FRANKIE. Are you on your own?

PUGH. Yeah

FRANKIE. Good

PUGH. Smudge is on the bus

FRANKIE. Okay

PUGH. Dan says he's not coming and Pidge is at A&E getting stitches in his face.

FRANKIE. He's. Stitches?

PUGH. Yeah. Some Latvian bloke threw an house brick at him.

FRANKIE. Why?

PUGH. Cos he's not Lithuanian, apparently

FRANKIE. Why's, right, why's, Dan…?

PUGH. Something about a night shift. Hong Kong hours.

FRANKIE. You've spoken to him?

PUGH. Yeah.

FRANKIE. When?

PUGH. He just phoned me a minute ago. Nothing like a bit of notice, eh?

FRANKIE checks his watch.

Nice watch. You going orienteering?

FRANKIE. I know. It's like we're fucking strangers.

PUGH. Eh?

FRANKIE. Kirsty bought it.

PUGH. I was only joking.

Beat.

FRANKIE. D'you ever feel like crying, Pugh?

PUGH....

FRANKIE. In a good way, when you look at Jenna?

PUGH....

FRANKIE. Cos your bones ache because it's just. Impossible, really, when you think about it, it's unbelievable that this this person's just been put so close – so nearby to you on the planet when there's billions, there's these billions of people in the world and this one person has been put close enough for you to to to to to to to meet and feel full up with and. Y'know? They could have been anywhere. But they're here, as if it's...

Beat.

Sorry. Ignore me, / I'm.

PUGH. No it's alright.

FRANKIE....

PUGH. I've never really thought about it. But.

Beat.

FRANKIE. But what? But yeah?

PUGH. Well.

Beat.

I suppose so. Yeah. Now you mention it.

FRANKIE. I think me and Kirsty might get married. Soon.

PUGH. Bloody hell!

FRANKIE. But that feeling. I get it. But not for.

Beat.

Not

PUGH. Who for then?

Beat.

FRANKIE. I've never cheated on her, Pugh

PUGH. No I know

FRANKIE. I couldn't do it, I mean I do. I've got this. Love. For her, and. Loads of it, really and, y'know, I sometimes think that that's. Enough, maybe. I mean, or maybe it should be enough, but then. Then I think about the future, and if I do – when I do think about it, the the future the, my future, if I dream about it – if I close my eyes and wish. If we can if we're allowed to do that, to live the way we want or at least try to, then, I mean…

Beat.

PUGH. You mean…?

FRANKIE. What's the point otherwise?

PUGH. Of what?

Long beat.

Listen.

FRANKIE....

PUGH. I dreamt of playing for West Ham

FRANKIE. I know

PUGH. Proper dreams. Running out at Upton Park, wearing the badge, clapping the fans. All that. And I worked really hard. Really hard

FRANKIE. I know you did

PUGH. But it didn't happen. And some nights I still dream about it.

FRANKIE. Yeah?

PUGH. Oh, mate.

Beat.

What's the point in that?

FRANKIE....

PUGH. I think ninety per cent of the time your dreams are to remind you you've fallen short.

FRANKIE. That's...

PUGH. Yeah. I know. It is. But then maybe that's life, eh?

Beat.

FRANKIE. Alright

PUGH. But look.

FRANKIE....

PUGH. I like Kirsty. A lot.

FRANKIE. I know

PUGH. But I only gave up on football cos I had to.

Beat.

This. For you. Well.

FRANKIE....

PUGH. There's no age limit, is there? So. Provided it's not the
   booze talking

FRANKIE. It's not.

PUGH. You're sure?

FRANKIE. Oh mate.

   Beat.

PUGH. Then…

FRANKIE. Thanks Pughie.

PUGH. Yeah.

   Beat.

   Happy birthday, eh?

   FRANKIE *smiles sadly.*

FRANKIE. Can we go to the pub please?

PUGH. Yeah. We'll be short anyway. Only a couple though, or
   you'll.

   Beat.

FRANKIE. What.

PUGH. No.

FRANKIE. What?

PUGH. I'm sure it's.

FRANKIE. What?

PUGH. No nothing, but.

   Beat.

   Did you say Kirsty's stopped drinking?

Seven

FRANKIE *and* KIRSTY *in the living room.*

KIRSTY. So?

FRANKIE. So.

KIRSTY. So you think I'm.

FRANKIE....

KIRSTY. How could I possibly be

FRANKIE. You tell me

KIRSTY. When that would require us / to

FRANKIE. Yeah

KIRSTY. To

FRANKIE. Yeah

KIRSTY. I mean we'd actually need / to

FRANKIE. Or not

KIRSTY. Which we – what?

FRANKIE. Not 'us'

KIRSTY. Not

FRANKIE. It doesn't require *us* to

KIRSTY. What are you talking about?

FRANKIE. Just you.

   Beat.

KIRSTY. Are you

FRANKIE. No?

KIRSTY. Are you fucking

FRANKIE....

KIRSTY. No! You

FRANKIE. Right

KIRSTY. How fucking dare you? How dare you?

FRANKIE. Then why weren't you

KIRSTY. What

FRANKIE. Why didn't / you

KIRSTY. You fucking

FRANKIE. The champagne

KIRSTY. ...

FRANKIE. You didn't, at dinner, at lunch, whatever, you / weren't

KIRSTY. Because I didn't want a drink! Not because I'm

FRANKIE. Fine

KIRSTY. What's so hard to believe – I had work to do Frankie, I've still got work to do – I didn't want some of your shit champagne, and you've decided

FRANKIE. No I just

KIRSTY. Like that's the more likely option of the two!

FRANKIE. Well, no

KIRSTY. What is the matter with you?

FRANKIE. Pugh said

KIRSTY. Pugh said? What the fuck does Pugh know?

FRANKIE. ...

KIRSTY. Does Pugh know we haven't had sex for nearly a year?

FRANKIE. ...

KIRSTY. No. I didn't think so.

FRANKIE. It's not.

Beat.

It's not that long, is / it?

KIRSTY. Yeah. It is.

Beat.

Who with then?

FRANKIE. What?

KIRSTY. Who am I supposed to have been with, / if

FRANKIE. No just

KIRSTY. Eh?

FRANKIE. No, forget I said it, / I'm

KIRSTY. No I don't want to forget, I want you to tell me

FRANKIE. No I'm / sorry

KIRSTY. Who am I supposed to have slept with, Frankie?

FRANKIE. Please

KIRSTY. Come on

FRANKIE. No leave it now

KIRSTY. No don't tell me to leave it

FRANKIE. Please, I'm sorry I said anything

KIRSTY. Well good! You fucking should be

FRANKIE. Let's just

KIRSTY. You are unbelievable. I can't believe you've got the nerve to accuse me / of

FRANKIE. I wasn't accusing you

KIRSTY. What would you call it?

FRANKIE....

KIRSTY. Frankie. We haven't had sex in a lifetime and you ask me if I'm pregnant? What would you call that?

FRANKIE. I'm sorry.

KIRSTY....

FRANKIE. I thought.

KIRSTY. I know what you thought

FRANKIE. I thought you might have been happier.

KIRSTY....

FRANKIE. With someone else, you might

KIRSTY. What's that supposed to mean?

Beat.

FRANKIE. Do you want to have sex?

KIRSTY. What, now?

FRANKIE. No, I mean

KIRSTY. After that?

FRANKIE. Not / now

KIRSTY. No!

FRANKIE. I just mean. With me. Any more.

Beat.

KIRSTY. You're lucky I haven't, Frankie.

FRANKIE....

KIRSTY. You're lucky I didn't

FRANKIE. Is that a yes or a no?

KIRSTY. Have you?

FRANKIE....

KIRSTY. Have you, is that why you're asking?

FRANKIE. No!

KIRSTY. Have you? If you have

FRANKIE. I haven't!

KIRSTY. Tell me, Frankie – if you've been with someone else

FRANKIE. I haven't. Ever. You know I haven't.

Beat.

KIRSTY. If I find out you're lying

FRANKIE. I'm not. I'm not, I'm really not, I'm, of course I'm not. I'm.

KIRSTY....

FRANKIE. I'm sorry.

Beat.

I just want

KIRSTY....

FRANKIE. I really fucking

KIRSTY. What. What do you want?

FRANKIE. I want to start again.

Beat.

Right back from the beginning. I want to go back to being kids and start again from the very beginning.

KIRSTY. Without me?

FRANKIE. No! No. No, no, just.

KIRSTY. Just?

FRANKIE. Not here. Somewhere else. / Somewhere

KIRSTY. Somewhere else

FRANKIE. Somewhere nice.

Long beat.

KIRSTY. I think you should go.

Beat.

Frankie I think you should go now please

FRANKIE. Go?

KIRSTY. Yeah

FRANKIE. Go where?

KIRSTY. You tell me. Somewhere nice. Anywhere, Frankie, I don't care, just go away now please get away from me right now actually, fuck off and don't come back until tomorrow or whenever it is you've decided that here is somewhere nice, where we live. Where our families are. Where our life is. Where we've done everything since the day we were born, when you've decided that here is nice enough for you then you can come back and apologise for everything you've said and accused me of and you can apologise for being a monumental prick. Alright?

Eight

FRANKIE *and* DAN *in the foyer of a city bank.*

DAN. Yeah, yeah, alright / yeah

FRANKIE. Just thought I'd.

DAN. …

FRANKIE. Come and say hello

DAN. Right. Nice.

FRANKIE. Is it?

DAN. What?

FRANKIE. Nice.

DAN. Well, yeah. I mean.

FRANKIE. Really?

DAN. How did you get here?

Beat.

FRANKIE. I tried calling you earlier. A couple of times. And I text you, / but.

DAN. Yeah, I was. It's doing this shift, I sleep at funny times so.

FRANKIE. Okay. Because I thought maybe…

DAN. No. No, it's. No.

FRANKIE. Okay.

Beat.

DAN. What are you.

FRANKIE....

DAN. Sort of. Doing here, Frankie?

FRANKIE. Oh, nothing. I was in the area, so.

DAN. Were you?

FRANKIE. Yeah.

DAN. In the area?

FRANKIE. Yeah. Well not like, not like, no. Not really, / but.

DAN. Right.

FRANKIE. Not the area but.

DAN. No.

FRANKIE. Y'know, I was.

DAN. You've been out then?

FRANKIE. Mmn?

DAN. Have you been out?

FRANKIE. Oh s– er – yeah, sort of. Yeah

DAN. You must've been / cos

FRANKIE. Somewhere

DAN. I mean it's

FRANKIE. Yeah

DAN. It's pretty late

FRANKIE. I know

DAN. With Kirsty, or...?

FRANKIE. What?

DAN. You. Out with.

FRANKIE. No. No on my own, really. Just

DAN. Right

FRANKIE. Quiet drink

DAN. Up town?

FRANKIE. Well

DAN. Till…

FRANKIE. I just thought

DAN. It's two o' clock.

FRANKIE. Is it?

DAN. Yeah it's. You're wearing a watch.

FRANKIE. I know, / but

DAN. You don't wear a watch.

Beat.

FRANKIE. No. I don't.

DAN. Look I can't… Hong Kong's just, the banks are opening now pretty much, / so

FRANKIE. No I won't. Keep you, or. I just thought maybe a talk.

DAN. A talk?

FRANKIE. A chat, yeah

DAN. Frank

FRANKIE. A word, a few words about

DAN. Mate, I'm

FRANKIE. Nnnn

DAN. I'm at work mate, Hong Kong's / just.

FRANKIE. Don't please, don't call me that.

Beat.

DAN. What?

FRANKIE. 'Mate', just.

DAN. Alright Frankie go home.

FRANKIE. No I'm just / I'm.

DAN. You're not 'just' anything.

FRANKIE. I am

DAN. You're drunk is what you are. You're drunk / and

FRANKIE. I'm not

DAN. You are, Frankie

FRANKIE. I am yeah I am, but that's not. That's. I just want a a a chat.

DAN. I'm at work, Frank

FRANKIE. Later then

DAN. I've only just. Look: I'll give you a call when I've got a minute, alright?

FRANKIE. Today?

DAN. What?

FRANKIE. Today. Will you call / today?

DAN. Yeah maybe yeah.

FRANKIE. Maybe or

DAN. Maybe, Frank. Maybe I will. Now please. Go home.

Beat.

FRANKIE. Alright.

DAN. Alright?

FRANKIE. I'm leaving Kirsty.

DAN. Why?

Beat.

Why, Frankie?

FRANKIE....

DAN. You haven't – have you said something?

FRANKIE. No

DAN. Have you?

FRANKIE. No

DAN. No?

FRANKIE. Not yet but I can't just

DAN. Yes. You can

FRANKIE. I can't. I can't Dan, honestly, I can't and it's not just now it's not because you're going away / or

DAN. You can't – Frank you can't fucking come to my work and. This is my work Frank, there's fucking people.

FRANKIE. So?

DAN. I mean what are you, what are we, fuck, Frank: what are you hoping for? Really?

FRANKIE. What am I.

DAN. Just. Go home.

FRANKIE. I could come with you.

DAN....

FRANKIE. To Hong Kong.

DAN. And do what? You're a roofer

FRANKIE. They've got roofs

DAN. Don't make me say it, Frankie

FRANKIE. What?

DAN....

FRANKIE. Say what?

Beat.

DAN. Go home.

FRANKIE. I told Kirsty. I told her how we came from the same grain of sand. How we walked out of the water together

DAN. What does that even mean? We're not the same, Frankie.

FRANKIE. We are, / that's

DAN. No we're not. All my life, my entire life I've been on the outside looking in –

FRANKIE. Me too.

DAN. You haven't! You fit. You belong, Frank.

FRANKIE. No / I

DAN. You do. You're confused, that's all.

FRANKIE. Don't tell / me

DAN. You're scared.

FRANKIE. I'm not

DAN. We're not kids any more – you make your choices and you stick by them – that's what you do now. You've made yours and so have I. And yeah. It's big. It's fucking big. It's forever big. But that's it. I'm going away, and I'm not coming back. That's it. So forget it – me and. Just go home. Or somewhere. Please. In another life, maybe. But not in this one, Frank.

FRANKIE. It might have been different if I'd come to uni, eh?

DAN. I doubt it

FRANKIE. I was close. I was really close.

DAN. It doesn't matter.

FRANKIE. You remember Peter Pan's? Holding my hand on the Barracuda?

DAN. This is what I mean; kids' stuff

FRANKIE. I wrote you a letter about it. My dad found it and put it on the fire.

DAN. Your / dad

FRANKIE. It's the only fight I've ever had.

DAN. Why are you telling me this?

FRANKIE. I wrote you a new one tonight. A letter

DAN. Keep it

FRANKIE. It's got a poem in it

DAN. I don't want it

FRANKIE. It's shit, but I meant it

DAN. Frank

FRANKIE. It fucking rhymes!

In his haste to get the letter out, FRANKIE*'s* (KIRSTY*'s*)
keys drop to the floor. He holds the letter out to DAN.

Will you read it? Please. That's all. Just. You can do what
you want – burn it after if you want, but. Please. Just. Once.
Just once. Before you go.

Beat.

DAN *takes the letter.*

Thank you.

DAN. I'm not just. This is for you too, Frankie.

FRANKIE. Yeah?

DAN. Yeah. It is, yeah. I'm looking out for both of us.

FRANKIE. Well. Thanks.

DAN. I'll see you, yeah?

FRANKIE. Yeah.

Beat.

Yeah.

Beat.

Yeah.

He picks up the keys from the floor, unsteadily.

Bye mate.

Nine

KIRSTY, *knackered, red-eyed, in bed, flicking through channels on the TV. We might just catch, from some low-rent advert:*

VOICE. Buy –

Before she's flicked on again, to the next homogenous TV sound bite.

And on, and on, until eventually she stops at a late-night travel-channel infomercial.

The inane details of a package holiday somewhere drift towards her.

She soaks it in for a little while. A dream of what might be.

Then she turns the TV off and picks up her phone.

Beat.

Puts it down again.

Long beat.

She picks up the phone again and checks the time. Then dials. Hits call.

And waits…

And waits…

Then the answerphone kicks in. She goes to speak…

KIRSTY.…

…but after what feels like a lifetime, decides not to say anything.

She hangs up.

Beat.

Then she put her phone down and turns out the light to sleep.

Darkness. Silence. Nothingness.

End.

Other Titles in this Series

A Nick Hern Book

So Here We Are first published in Great Britain in 2015 as a paperback original by Nick Hern Books Limited, The Glasshouse, 49a Goldhawk Road, London W12 8QP, in association with HighTide Festival Theatre and the Royal Exchange Theatre, Manchester

So Here We Are copyright © 2015 Luke Norris

Luke Norris has asserted his right to be identified as the author of this work

Cover image: Magnum Photos

Designed and typeset by Nick Hern Books, London
Printed in Great Britain by CPI Group (UK) Ltd

A CIP catalogue record for this book is available from the British Library

ISBN 978 1 84842 509 5

www.nickhernbooks.co.uk

 facebook.com/nickhernbooks

 twitter.com/nickhernbooks